Wakefield Press

F.J. Gillen's
First Diary 1875

F.J. Gillen's diary was written in ink, in a small A6 black covered notebook. The diary was located during the 1970s at the South Australian Museum among the papers of the Adelaide psychiatrist and anthropologist, H.K. Fry, to whom the diary had been lent by Gillen's son, J.B. Gillen. This transcription was made by Francis Gillen's grandson, Dr Robert Gillen, from a copy made available by Philip Jones of the South Australian Museum.

F. J. Gillen's
First Diary 1875

Adelaide to Alice Springs
March to June

Edited by
ROBERT S. GILLEN

Wakefield Press
16 Rose Street
Mile End
South Australia 5031
www.wakefieldpress.com.au

First published 1995
This edition published 2019

Cover designed by Liz Nicholson, Wakefield Press
Typeset by Clinton Ellicott, Adelaide

ISBN 978 1 74305 685 1

A catalogue record for this book is available from the National Library of Australia

Wakefield Press thanks Coriole Vineyards for continued support

Contents

Friday April 16th 1875

Turned out 8 am. fine day – [illegible] salting sheep & getting everything ready for a start tomorrow – Getting quite used to camping out & find it is a deal more comfortable in a civilized habitation – Myriads of flies about & find them awfully troublesome – They appear to be a different species to the common fly seen about Adelaide but are far more troublesome –

Bob & I laid it out in the waggon all [illegible] [illegible] our minds by reading smoking &c.

Got to Bed about 9

Foreword

F.J. Gillen's 'First Campaign in the Bush'

Philip Jones

Head, Division of Anthropology, South Australian Museum

Given Francis Gillen's own modesty, his remote location and his relatively early death at the age of fifty-seven it is understandable that his career as an anthropologist has been overshadowed by that of the scientist, museum director, art patron and academic, Walter Baldwin Spencer. For his part, Spencer assiduously gave Gillen his due in each of their joint publications and recorded his debt to the Central Australian telegraph station master on many separate occasions. Spencer's encouragement and guidance were fundamental to Gillen's achievements, both as an anthropologist and as a photographer. That said, Gillen's contributions in these fields reveal a depth of insight and originality which have been overlooked until recently. His career is long overdue for reassessment.

Gillen published three anthropological papers in his own right, six joint papers (five with Spencer) and six co-authored books with Spencer (four posthumous). Despite the breadth of understanding of Aboriginal social systems and religious life

FIELD, HANLEY, P. SQUIRE, F. GILLEN,
JACK BESLEY, E. SQUIRE – GILLEN'S COLLEAGUES,
ALICE SPRINGS TELEGRAPH OPERATORS
(LIGHTNING SQUIRTERS), C. 1895

represented in these publications, Gillen's reputation has remained as the genial, whisky-drinking foil to Spencer's brilliant academic persona. The 1968 facsimile publication of *The Camp Jottings of F.J. Gillen*, his edited account of the 1901–1902 expedition with Spencer, probably embellished this view; its deft and amusing vignettes of the episodes and trials of expedition life cast its author as a lesser intellect than the 'Professor'.

In its self-deprecatory Irishness, Gillen's resilient humour is as evident in this first journal as it is in *Camp Jottings*. The setbacks and disadvantages confronted by Gillen during his subsequent career as a frontier official provided a fertile source for this wry humour; there is even room for the suggestion that his modesty allowed, possibly even invited, the official and critical neglect which affected his career as a telegraph station master and his longer-term reputation as as an anthropologist.

The publication of this slim journal may not directly affect those perceptions of Gillen, but it will help us to gain a new perspective on his later evolution of one of Australia's most remarkable social researchers. It will also help to place in context Gillen's 150 fascinating letters to Spencer, written between 1894 and 1912, the year of Gillen's death. These incisive and sophisticated conjectures about Aboriginal life and custom are soon to be published for the first time; they provide a radical contrast to the raw and naive experiences documented in this first journal.

Gillen worked in the telegraph stations of Central Australia for twenty-five years. His lifeline and that of his fellows was the Overland Telegraph Line itself – a thread of European communication which bisected hundreds of intangible but meaningful lines of Aboriginal song-poetry and ancestral paths. It is one of the ironies of Australian bush life that the 'lightning squirters' or telegraph operators, like the Aboriginal people themselves, were able to communicate effectively across enormous distances with each other, yet rarely across cultures.

Few would have been aware of this irony; Gillen himself never remarked upon it. His consciousness of the social and religious connections which laced across the continent was to become as refined as that of any European of his day, yet this awareness was hard-earned. Many other telegraph station men were oblivious to the complexities and subtleties of Aboriginal life; they saw only a gradual deterioration in a pristine and primitive culture, rather than the efforts of Aborigines to engage with and accommodate European culture. Gillen also brought with him such preconceptions of Aborigines as a primitive, unchanging and backward people. His 1875 journal is peppered with evidence that he, too, regarded the Aborigines as marginal to European progress and achievements.

The extraordinary value of this youthful account lies in our knowledge that Gillen altered these perceptions radically, not only for himself, but for European Australia. Without Gillen's insight and the opportunities which he took to comprehend and work his way inside the mental culture of Aboriginal Australia, this culture would have remained opaque to Europeans for a good deal longer.

Judged by today's standards, Gillen's casual descriptions of Aborigines as 'niggers', and his various characterisations of them as indolent and marginal figures, are undoubtedly racist and patronising. He continued to use these terms throughout his time in Central Australia, for twenty-five years. So did a great many Europeans, including several whose support for Aboriginal causes is unquestioned. There were no unblemished champions in any camp on the outback frontiers. The point is that Gillen was perceived as an ally by Aboriginal people themselves in the region, particularly for his actions in arresting police-trooper W.H. Willshire following several murders of Aboriginal people in reprisal for cattle killing. This controversial act, together with Gillen's genuine and intelligent curiosity about social and religious life, convinced Aboriginal people that he could be trusted with their secrets and, in many cases, their sacred objects. This trust was, in most part, respected by him.

This first journal contains crucial evidence that Gillen's interest in Aboriginal culture would expand in later years. The journal includes two word lists, apparently collected by him at two separate localities. From slight circumstantial evidence in the journal, it would appear that the first list was collected at or south of Peake Station, not far south of present-day Oodnadatta. This list contains mainly Arabana words, and possibly some Wangkangurru, a related language spoken through the Simpson Desert to the east. After Peake Station, Gillen's next close contact with Aboriginal people was near the Hugh River on 3 June, 1875. He described the visitors to the camp as of the 'Coomarrie tribe', understandably mistaking the Aranda kinship term *kumarre* for a tribal name. It is likely that the second vocabulary, copied into the back of the journal, was obtained here, particularly as one of the men 'could speak a few words of English'. This vocabulary, allowing for Gillen's individual phonetic transcription, has been identified as mainly Southern Aranda, and closely matches a vocabulary collected by Gillen at Charlotte Waters Telegraph Station and published by him in 1886.

Gillen's developing career as an anthropologist has never been adequately examined. His 1886 contribution to Edward Curr's massive survey of Aboriginal languages and customs has, until now, been assumed as the first stage in this career, which was considerably advanced by his chapter in the 1896 Horn Expedition Report, and still further by his joint publication with Spencer in 1899 of *The Native Tribes of Central Australia.* This first journal tells us that his anthropological career in fact began almost from the moment he reached Peake Station, a point acknowledged to represent the frontier of Aboriginal–European contact. Travellers from that point were advised to carry weapons, but Gillen (who never carried a gun) began collecting Aboriginal vocabularies. It was to be another two decades before the first phase of Central Australian exploration was considered to be complete. In fact, 1875 was an important year for exploration, and Gillen's party encountered both Ernest Giles and Percival E. Warburton at different stages. Through these meetings, and the experience of passing by at least five 'perishes' – graves of travellers who had succumbed to the bush – Gillen must have been continually reminded of the fragility of the Overland Telegraph Line's presence and of his own future prospects. No doubt this consciousness accounts, in part at least, for the tone of bravado in the young man's journal.

Gillen's famous partnership with Spencer was struck casually through their meeting at the end of the 1894 Horn Scientific Expedition which Spencer had accompanied as zoologist. Spencer delayed his departure from Alice Springs and spent several weeks as the guest of the convivial Gillen and his family, discussing natural science and anthropology in Gillen's smoke-filled and artefact-decorated den. The youthful Gillen's 1875 journal gives some insight into the ease with which this relationship was forged. His capacity for making wry but invariably cheerful observations on each adversity which confronted him during his long journey north from Adelaide would certainly have endeared him to most of his companions, even if his garrulity may have tried others occasionally.

Gillen's 1875 journal provides other hints of his later capacities. His moral advice to his 'metropolitan friends' and later travellers which closes the account is an early example of his ability to succinctly extract the content from an experience and to summarise it for others. It was this capacity which made Gillen such a powerful and influential anthropological source and informant for Spencer. His homily is a sturdy blend of pragmatism and idealism; perhaps if Gillen were to have penned it afresh, twenty-five years later, he might have made reference to more subtle influences, if not to the songs and ancestral paths which criss-crossed beneath the single strand of wire connecting the Centre with the world. All this, and a profound awareness of the Centre's natural and human history, lay ahead of the young telegraph operator.

FRANCIS JAMES GILLEN,
AGED NINETEEN

Preface

Robert Spencer Gillen
MB BS Adelaide, DPM (RCP&S) London, FRANZCP

This diary is the story of a journey from Adelaide to Alice Springs made by a nineteen-year-old young man in 1875. From this beginning he became fascinated with the culture of the indigenous people and subsequently, with Sir Baldwin Spencer, co-authored *The Native Tribes of Central Australia*, which was published by Macmillan in 1899 and became a classic in the study of anthropology.

Francis James Gillen was born somewhere in the vicinity of Cavan, near Adelaide, in South Australia. His birth was registered in the Little Para Post Office on 28 October 1855. His parents, Thomas and Brigid (nee McCann) Gillen, were married in County Cavan, Ireland on 13 January 1855. They set sail from Plymouth in Cornwall on 28 March 1855, on the sailing ship *Sea Park*. They arrived at Port Adelaide on 25 June 1855.

Little is known of Francis's early life, except that his family moved to Clare, north of Adelaide, because his father couldn't stand the call of the local bush curlew, which he feared was like the banshee, which to an Irishman was a female spirit whose wailing warned of impending death.

Francis began to earn his own living at the age of eleven; he joined the Public Service as a telegraph messenger in Clare on 15 January 1867, earning £30 a year. What is known about Gillen in this employment comes from an unpublished diary of Arthur Treloar. The date is January, 1878.

I rode on to Finniss (Springs) in two days, the last day I was joined by F.J. Gillen, telegraph operator at Alice Springs whom I had known well as a lad when he would be sent to Watervale to relieve the operator there – and a cheeky little fellow he was. I once helped to take him out of a hole in the Skilly Creek. A lot of lads were having a holiday and spent it cray-fishing in the Skilly, below Hughes Park. Gillen was with us and it was decided that we should have a swim. Gillen said he could swim and it was not until we (J. Bills – since, Mayor of Laura – and myself) were called to by another lad, that we noticed him struggling in the water. We were on the opposite bank and, by the time we reached him, he had sunk twice. J. Bills reached him first and caught him by the hair and between us we took him to the bank and, after throwing up a lot of water, he soon got right.

When he was fifteen, Gillen was transferred to Adelaide as a junior assistant at £80 p.a. From this time he received some education, studying at night at the School of Mines. He used to tell a story of his early days in Adelaide when he was a raw youth from the country who knew nothing of the laws of the corporation. One day while walking through Victoria Square, which was then a mere paddock, with a few poorly kept flower beds, he plucked a nice bunch of chrysanthemums, under the impression that they were grown there for the benefit of the public. A police officer caught him in the act, and the youngster readily accompanied him to the watchhouse, which was situated next to the Criterion Hotel. To his surprise he was detained for having committed an illegal offence. An officer of the Post Office was dispatched to explain that the lad had acted in an innocent way and plead for his forgiveness. The police granted the necessary pardon, and the Clare boy was allowed to resume his work without having to answer a formal charge.

In the early 1870s, the construction of the Overland Telegraph Line ensured rapid promotion for those in the Service who were prepared to serve in the Northern Territory. Gillen's interest was not diminished by the fact that he was the operator on duty in the Adelaide Office when the Barrow Creek Station, in the Northern Territory, was attacked by Aborigines in February 1874, and station master John L. Stapleton mortally wounded. In his diary of 1901, Gillen wrote:

Stapleton received a spear in the groin and lived a few brief hours knowing he was mortally wounded. He had a wife and bairns in Adelaide and to me, as operator in the Adelaide office, fell the painful duty of conducting a telegraphic conversation between the dying man on the Barrow and his heart-broken wife in Adelaide.

In 1875, Gillen was posted to the Overland Telegraph Line at Alice Springs as an operator at £120 p.a. He left Adelaide on Good Friday, 26 March 1875, and commenced the journey described in this diary.

Gillen was an operator on various stations of the O.T.L.

from 1 May 1875 to 1 December 1892, when he was promoted to Post and Telegraph Master of Alice Springs at £270 p.a. His duties gave him control of the line from Oodnadatta in the south to Attack Creek (recorded in the annals of John McDouall Stuart) in the north. He eventually became known as the 'Pooh-Bah of Way Back' or the 'Pontiff', such was his standing.

In his capacity as a government official, Gillen often came in contact with the indigenous people of the area. This was initially forced on him by their habit of breaking off the insulators along the line to fashion their traditional implements – a problem he soon solved by giving them his empty whiskey bottles. This diary reflects his initial prejudices, which were common ones in the era. It is also clear that he was more interested in the Aboriginal people than were most of his travelling companions. Over the ensuing years, he developed a deep affection and regard for them and learned their language. He was trusted to such an extent that he was admitted as a fully initiated member of the Aranda tribe. They called him the 'Oknirrabata'; which means 'great teacher', an honour that enabled him to attend ceremonies and be given information about tribal law and rituals that no one but an initiated member of the tribe could witness or discuss. In an interview given to the *Register* newspaper of 12 September 1899, he said:

I never carried a revolver, the native is a natural reader of character. He can tell by your face whether you are genuine or a humbug, and acts accordingly. It is always best to act squarely with him and he pretty quickly finds it out, for in his native wilds, the darkie is no fool. He also said: *The Australian black is very sensitive to ridicule, and if he thinks the white man talking to him is playing with him, or seeking idly to find out something about his customs, he will cleverly evade all enquiry, but if he thinks that he is being dealt with as man-to-man he is not a bad fellow. What the blackfellow respects in the white man is courage and the truth.*

Gillen's concern for the care of local Aranda people led to his confrontation with a mounted constable, William Willshire, who was condemned by some and praised by others for the way he conducted his duties. On 22 February 1891 Willshire raided a native camp and ordered his two native policemen, Larry and Joe, to shoot two men, Roger and Donkey. Due to Gillen's intervention, Willshire was arrested on 29 April, charged with murder and committed to stand trial in Port Augusta. He was acquitted because of lack of evidence, and Gillen received a bad press for his trouble. In the book *Willshire of Alice Springs* by Austin Stapleton, it was said, 'Mr Gillen J.P., who had lived so many years amongst the blacks, must have known that their words were about as reliable as so many lunatics'. However, Gillen's reputation was enhanced amongst the Aranda elders by his firm actions, and they gave him increased respect.

1891 was a busy year for Gillen because, with a little bit of help from some of his colleagues, he managed to wed. On 5 August 1891, he married Amelia Maude Besley in Mount Gambier. His wife's brother, step-brother and cousin were on the staff of the O.T.L. and were all great friends. Francis's and Amelia's families may have known each other earlier, as her father had been a teacher at Sevenhill College, Clare. Mr Besley was an accomplished musician, and so was his daughter, who took her piano to Alice Springs and entertained the many people who visited the Telegraph Station. Amelia had her first child in Mount Gambier, catching the train there from Oodnadatta – after a trip by sulky from Alice Springs that normally took anything from two to three weeks, depending on the weather. A description of what this train journey was like is given in the book *Alice on the Line* by Doris Blackwell and Douglas Lockwood: 'our train had no sleeping cars, so we stopped each night at an hotel and the train waited for us until after breafast next day.' Amelia remained in Alice Springs for her next confinement. Gillen, writing to Baldwin Spencer[1] in February 1895 said: 'I am glad to say both wife and little one are doing splendidly – I feel rather out in the cold myself. The house is dominated by a Sarey Gamp-like person whom I imported from down country some months ago.' This woman's name was Mrs Connor. According to Douglas Lockwood, it was later discovered that she had gone to Alice Springs in order to be as far away as she could from regular supplies of whiskey. When she left the Gillens she got only as far as Oodnadatta before her alcoholism began again.

The family myth has it that the Gillen's second child, John, was the first white male born in Alice Springs – which is difficult to prove or disprove. The first white child born in Alice Springs was probably Lucelle (Lulu) Benstead, born in Stuart Town (now Alice Springs), in 1891.

This first diary shows Gillen's early interest in Aboriginal people, which developed into a guiding motive of his life. In an article in the *Register* of 7 December 1898, he was reported to have explained that:

he had always liked the blackfellow as he was to be found before being contaminated with white races and habits. Situated as he had been for many years, in Central Australia, he had had every opportunity of acquiring knowledge concerning him. He did not however, seriously undertake to study him from a scientific point of view until advised by Dr. Stirling and Lord Kintore and also Professor Spencer, who visited Alice Springs with the Horn Expedition in 1894. The latter gentleman especially encouraging him and promising to collaborate with him in the publication of a book on the subject. After that he set to work in real earnest, and collected, and committed to paper, a great deal of information. Professor Spencer came up to Alice Springs some years after.

Thus began a synergistic relationship between Francis Gillen and Baldwin Spencer that produced some of the classic writings

~

1 Sir Walter Baldwin Spencer (1860–1929) was born in Lancashire, England. He was educated at Oxford University where he studied evolutionary biology under Professor H.N. Moseley and attended lectures by Ruskin and E.B. Tylor. In 1866 he applied for the foundation chair of Biology at the University of Melbourne and developed it into a major centre of research. He had many interests including being a patron of the arts, President of the V.F.L., and scientific exploration. In 1894 the Horn expedition to Central Australia recruited Spencer as zoologist and photographer. This expedition rekindled his anthropological interest when he met F.J. Gillen. Their combined efforts caused Sir James Frazer to say in 1899 – 'In immortalising the native tribes of Central Australia, Spencer and Gillen, have immortalised themselves.'

about Aboriginal people. On July 12, 1897, Professor Spencer wrote to Frazer[2]:

My friend Mr. Fison has kindly sent on to me your letter, in which you make enquiries with regard to the joint work of Mr. Gillen and myself. First let me say that the work which we are doing is due in the first instance to Mr. Gillen. He had for some years been taking a great interest in the Central Australian natives, and the result of his work up to the time when we met has already been published in the report of the Horn Expedition to Central Australian, Vol IV. At the close of that expedition, I spent some time with him, and having been originally interested in matters anthropological by my old teacher Prof. Moseley, and also by Dr. Tylor[3]*, was able to suggest to him, lines of enquiry with regard to Totems and other matters of interest*[4].

Sometimes Spencer and Gillen worked together in the field during Spencer's university vacations. At other times Gillen would investigate alone and wire his results to Spencer, who corresponded with Frazer. Frazer checked their work, directed further avenues of enquiry, and taught them the discipline of anthropology. It was Frazer who read the final draft of their writings and organised the publication of their book, *The Native Tribes of Central Australia*, in 1899. It became a classic work of Australian anthropology, and has been read and quoted by all serious anthropologists interested in aboriginal cultures from that time to the present.

Gillen's contribution to this work was sometimes under-valued by academics, his superiors in the Public Service and the press, and Spencer always tried to correct the impression. On one occasion the following appeared in the the press:

On this matter we have received the following telegram from Professor Spencer, dated Alice Springs, December 26, in which he says, 'As paragraph appearing in Chronicle, December 12, may convey the wrong impression, would you kindly state that Mr. Gillen and myself are engaged on joint work on Central Australian natives in continuation of work already done by Mr. Gillen. Mr. F. Gillen, the Inspector of Overland Telegraphs who is referred to is a brother of the late Commissioner of Crown Lands and has obtained a large amount of information regarding the customs of the aborigines'.

Gillen spent twenty-four years in the interior and during his time in Alice Springs, as well as his Overland Telegraph Line duties, he was a Sub-Protector of Aborigines and a Special Magistrate. On his farewell from Alice Springs on 29 April, 1899, the *Register* newspaper reported that 'he was thanked for his constant acts of kindness to the members of his staff as well as to the public generally. His skill in medicine being especially

~

2 Professor James G. Frazer (1854–1941) was born in Scotland and was a Cambridge Fellow for sixty two years. Among other books, he wrote *The Golden Bough*, a vast study of ancient mythology, the first work in English to understand the religion of classical antiquity in the context of primitive religion. The influence of his work had wide ranging implications for modern anthropology, classics, cultral history and folklore.

3 Sir Edward Burrell Tylor (1832–1917). In his book *Primitive Culture*, 1871, he introduced the terms 'animism' and 'fetishism' into anthropology.

4 Spencer's Scientific Correspondence with Sir James Frazer and others (Clarendon Press), 1932.

attended to – he has been physical surgeon and dispensing chemist for the interior for many years.' Family myth has it that he once amputated the leg of a man while receiving step-by-step instructions via telegraph from a Dr Stirling[5].

He had given up two major inducements to leave the Centre and stayed to continue his anthropological work after being encouraged by Spencer to remain. When he needed to move because his family were growing up and needed education, he was denied a city position and was sent to Moonta instead, and both the local and city press wondered why he was being denied recognition by his superiors. In January 1899 he and his family moved to Moonta where he was the Post-Master and he soon threw himself energetically into the affairs of the town and became president of various societies and clubs, including the golf club, where he was remembered more for the originality of his language than for his score on the course.

In 1900 a petition was sent by scientific societies in England to the South Australian and Victorian governments to release Gillen and Spencer from their official duties for a year so they could continue their ethnological researches through the centre of Australia to the Gulf of Carpentaria. Permission was soon granted by both governments, and Spencer and Gillen were given a year's leave of absence on full pay. The cost of the expedition was borne partly by Mr David Syme of Melbourne, the proprietor of the Melbourne *Age*, who gave £1000. Spencer's father, Ruben, and the Victorian government each gave an additional £500. The South Australian government presented them with a team of four horses and the express vehicle used by Lord Kintore on his expeditions through the continent in 1891, and provided them with free railway accommodation. They left Oodnadatta on 19 March 1900. F.J. Gillen's diary of this expedition was published by the Libraries Board of South Australia in 1968 as *The Camp Jottings of F.J. Gillen. The Northern Tribes of Central Australia*, a co-authored companion book to *The Native Tribes of Central Australia*, was published after the expedition in 1904 by Macmillan and recieved enthusiastic reviews from the international academic and popular press.

Gillen was not a businessman. He dabbled in shares, but nearly every gold mine he invested in finished up not being worth the paper the scrip was printed on. He was always poor. On his visits to Adelaide he hobnobbed with the rich and the famous, dining with the Bonythons, Sir Samuel Way or Angas Johnston and others who entertained him at the Adelaide Club. He would return home and worry about whether he could afford to send his children to good schools and wonder why the authorities would not create a postion for him in the city when he was lauded by the press for his ethnographical experience and the lectures he gave. In a letter to Spencer in February

~

5 Dr Edward Charles Stirling was born at Strathalbyn, South Australia in1848. He was a distinguished surgeon, scientist, museum director and politician and in 1886 he introuduced a Bill to enfranchise women. He was medical officer and anthropologist with W.A. Horn Expedition and wrote the anthropological section published as the record of the expedition's discoveries and included the notes of F.J. Gillen's observations and photographs.

1902, he wrote about his superior Sir Charles Todd[6], the Post-Master General:

Todd was too unwell, he said, to attend the lecture. The old beggar didn't say one word by way of congratulation, which rather nettled me. Millionaire Brookman gave a lunch on Friday to celebrate the 40th anniversary of Stuart planting the flag on North Coast. Four survivors of the party were there including a nice modest fellow, a surveyor named Stephen King. I sat opposite to Todd and I fancy the old chap did not approve of his subordinate being placed in such close proximity to him. I had a long chat with him in the morning on official matters and he distinctly promised to recommend me for appointment to the first big office becoming vacant about the city, so this is satisfactory if he doesn't forget all about it. I told him that I thought my long service in the Interior and my ethnological work entitled me to some special consideration at the hands of the Government and he was good enough to say that was his opinion. By the way, I must tell you that the little acting Governor's last words to me were: 'I should like to see the Federal Government give you a decent salary and free you from your present duties so that you could devote the whole of your time to ethnographical research'. I told him that they were far more likely to reduce my present salary.

Although Gillen was read, and quoted, by an international audience (including Sigmund Freud)[7] for the rest of his life he was kept in the obscurity of a minor country post office position. Todd, who he accompanied on this journey to Alice Springs, did forget Gillen's request and kept him subordinate to the end.

Gillen died from the effects of an obscure progressive muscle-wasting disease – amyotropic lateral sclerosis – in 1912 aged fifty-six, leaving a widow and five children. His eldest son, Brian, was accidentally killed a short time before Gillen's death. Gillen's wife was left penniless when he died. She could not understand why Spencer received all the credit and was wealthy to boot. In a fit of pique she bundled up all Spencer's letters to Gillen (with the exception of two) and burnt them. Luckily all Gillen's letters to Spencer have survived and are to be published in 1995.

Spencer went on and published two further books in both their names, the two volume *Across Australia* and the two volume *The Arunta* and thereafter published in his own name. Wherever or whenever the humanities are discussed in scientific circles, the name of F.J. Gillen will always be remembered as a man who was one of the first to recognise, respect and record the true worth of Australian Aboriginal people.

R.S.G., Adelaide 1995

~

6 Sir Charles Todd (1826–1910). Born in London, he trained and worked as an astronomer and then in galvanic electricity, the basis of early electric telegraphs. In 1855 he was appointed the government astronomer and superintendent of telegraphs for South Australia and supervised construction of the colony's first local and interstate telegraphs. He suggested that the Adelaide–Darwin line should be built to speed communications with Europe, linking with the undersea cable to Singapore. However, it took ten years for work to begin, in 1870, by which time Todd was Post-Master General of South Australian and was also organising the Adelaide–Perth telegraph. He had planned the Overland Telegraph work so well that it took only two years to complete the line, opening in 1872. Surveyors named Alice Springs after his wife, and named the Todd River, which flows through the township, after him. He was knighted in 1893 and continued his astronomical as well as his post office work, modernising the Adelaide observatory and receiving numerous honours from learned societies.

7 *Totem and Taboo* (Routledge and Kegan Paul), 1950.

Editor's note – I wish to thank the following organisations and individuals who generously answered my questions and helped in other ways.

Clare Regional History Group; Australian Railways Historical Society, South Australian Division; Mr Gerald Fischer; Mr John Bagot; Mr John M. Tregenza; Jacquie Shannon Gillen; Messrs Robert Thornton and G. Wagner, Adelaide City Council Archives; Mortlock Library of South Australiana; Lady Downer; Mr Steven Ronayne, Aptos Cruz Galleries; Emeritus Professor D.J. Mulvaney; Mr Michael Kempe; Norman McKenzie and Bill Stevens of the History Trust of South Australia.

This diary would not have been published without the caring, coaching, correcting and contributing of that walking encyclopaedia of Australian history – Richard Kimber. I am most grateful for his generosity, interest and attention to detail and I am greatly in his debt.

I am grateful also to Philip Jones of the South Australian Museum, whose contribution and discipline have been invaluable. Any errors that do remain are entirely my own responsibility.

Thanks to Michael Bollen and all at Wakefield Press for their tolerance and help in educating me in the discipline of publishing.

Special thanks are due to my secretary, Mrs Christine James, for her patience, tolerance and cheerfulness in getting the job done.

R.S.G.

The Diary

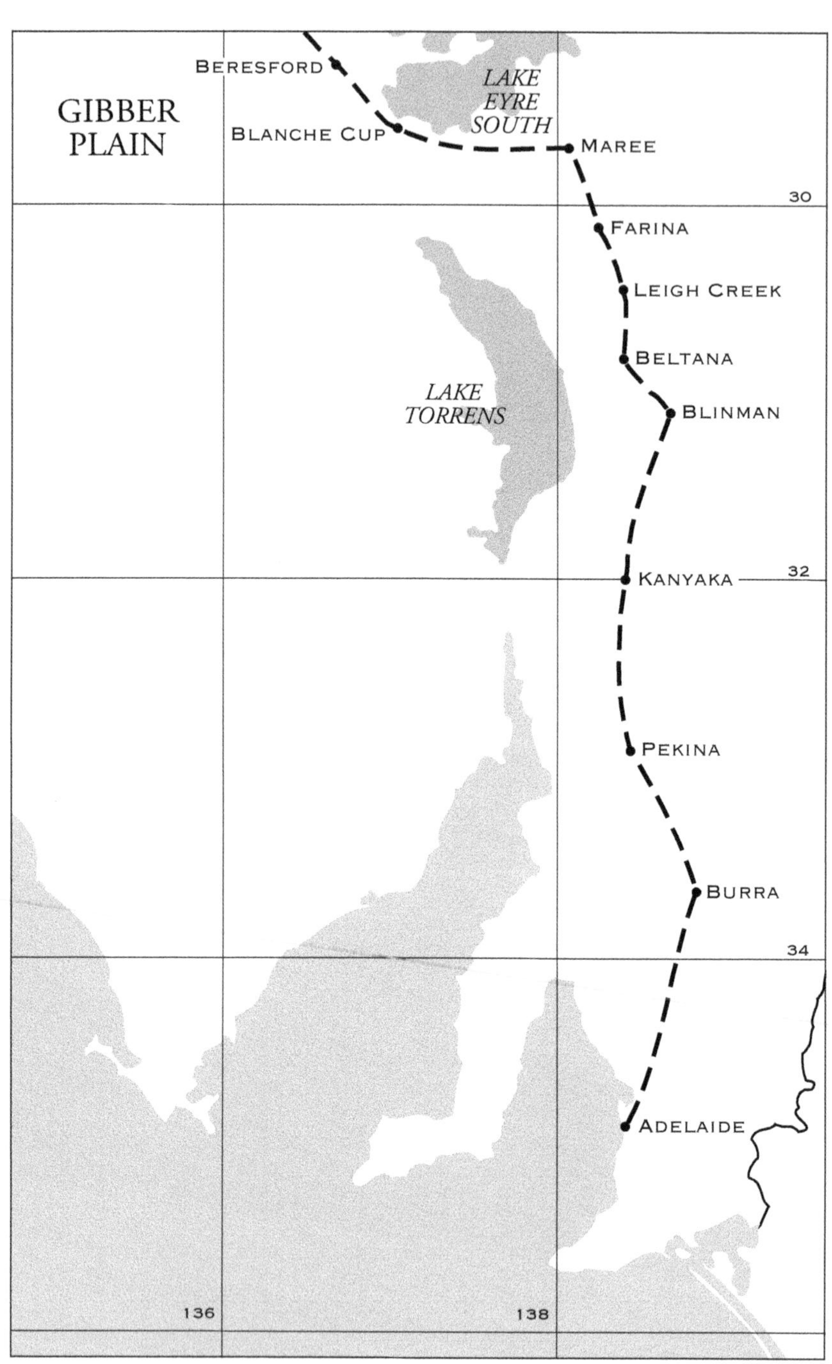

BERESFORD
GIBBER PLAIN
BLANCHE CUP
LAKE EYRE SOUTH
MAREE
30
FARINA
LEIGH CREEK
BELTANA
LAKE TORRENS
BLINMAN
KANYAKA
32
PEKINA
BURRA
34
ADELAIDE
136
138

GOOD FRIDAY, MARCH 26TH ~ Left Adelaide per train for Burra[1] at 4.30. Started from Redruth[2] for Blinman[3] at 11.30 pm. Our first halt was at Booborowie[4] Eating House, a distance of 17 miles from Redruth, where we had the pleasure of paying 6[d] a cup for some wishwash called Coffee, by the Landlady, had to patronise the Rum bottle to wash it down. Changed horses and away, Breakfasted at Canowie[5] 4 am, made a good feed, don't think the Landlady made much out of me! Reached Yattina[6] 8.15, here we got some beer, the first we tasted since leaving Redruth. I may mention it was procured at a Sly Grog Shop and like stolen fruit it was much relished by all hands. Rum bottle nearly exhausted by this time, so took a few bottles of Beer with us, they did not keep though, it being hot weather. My friend McClure[7] displayed great anxiety on

~

1 Burra – In 1875, The Great Northern Railway ended at Burra. It reached Quorn on 15/12/1879, Maree on 7/2/1884, Oodnadatta on 7/1/1891 and Alice Springs on 2/8/1929. The place name 'Burra' has been the subject of almost endless controversy in regard to its derivation. The mines are named the Burra Burra Mines from their being situated near the creek of that name. In the local Aboriginal language the word 'burra' means 'great', but some people believe it was named by local Hindustani labourers from the Hindustani word which means 'great'.
2 Redruth – named after a town and parish of that designation in East Cornwall. Its adoption in the locality of the Burra may be due to the fact that Captain Henry Roach, manager of the Burra Copper Mine until the early fifties, arrived from the Cornish Redruth in 1846.
3 Blinman – The copper mine was discovered by Robert Blinman, a shepherd employed on the Angorichina run.
4 Booboorowie – Aboriginal name for round waterhole.
5 Canowie – from Kanyaowie – water hole in the rock.
6 Yattina – The town was proclaimed on 16 July, 1874. The Aboriginal name for a black rock in the vicinity.
7 McClure – Bob, a workmate.

that point. Arrived at Pekina[8] about 11 am, had a tolerably good feed of Salt horse[9] which made us most infernally thirsty. Purchased a six Chambered shooting Iron from a German Fellow Passenger whom I named Bismarch[10],
he took to the nickname very Kindly. Awfully dry drive between Yattina and Kanyaka[11], very little water to be got and all our liquor exhausted. Reached latter-mentioned place about 7.30 pm, had a feed of roast Goat (the Landlord assured us it was mutton, if so it was infernally tough). Shipped a good cargo of medical comforts[12] and retired to a virtuous couch for a snooze. Up again at 3 am and proceeded on our journey. About 10 miles beyond Kanyaka lost the cup off one of the naves[13]. This *terrible* accident detained us some time, after half an hours fruitless search for the missing Cup, had to make a makeshift. Breakfasted at Carsons Crossing. Find Coach Travelling has a strange affect [sic] on human Nature. Colleen Bawns[14] the order of the day throughout the journey. Arrived at Wilpena[15] just in Time for Dinner, did my duty to the good things provided, one dish being a Shoulder of Tough old Goat. Between here and Blinman had three Breakdowns – but nothing serious. Arrived at Blinman 7.20 pm Sunday, thoroughly Knocked up. So much for our journey by Terry's Royal Mail[16] drawn by nothing better than a lot of warmed-up Skeletons.
I forgot to mention that we passed the Grave of an old Bushman who died on the road, and was buried about 30 yards from the Bank of the Devil's Crossing – this is the Crossing over a dry River, the name I forget.

At Blinman met with a most extraordinary Specimen of human nature, in the Shape of a negro whose mouth extended from one side of the face to the other, he Could comfortably take my fist in his enormous Cavity but would much rather take in pennies.

MONDAY THE 29TH – EASTER MONDAY ~ Find Blinman Township a miserable hole, one bad feature in the place is that we have to pay 6^{d} for every liquor from Ginger pop down to Common Run down – Fine Beer brewed in the Township. People keep the Holiday on Tuesday, on account of Monday being their Mail day. Bob and self invited to stay for an evening party on Tuesday made arrangements to stay another

~

8 Pekina – presumed local Aboriginal place name – 'ina' means water, 'Pek' unknown.
9 Salt horse – salted beef.
10 Bismarch [sic] – Otto von Bismarck – 19th century soldier-stateman, largely responsible for the unification of Germany.
11 Kanyaka – Kanyaka Station took its name from the Aboriginal word applied to a conspicuous rock. The name was corrupted from Adenyaka, meaning 'the place of stone'. The original station was developed by Hugh Proby, the third son of an Admiral who served under Nelson. Hugh Proby was drowned when he was 24 and his grave is a few kilometres beyond Quorn.
12 medical comforts – liquor.
13 nave – the block of a wheel, into which the end of the axle-tree is inserted and from which the spokes radiate.
14 Colleen Bawn – An erection. Rhyming slang, Colleen Bawn = horn.
15 Wilpena – there are two possible meanings for this Aboriginal word. (1) meaning a 'place of bent fingers' and (2) the word 'wilpi' was widely used for a 'wurli' meaning a camping shelter. E.M. Bagot is credited with the discovery of the Pound in 1850, while John McLeay claimed that he was the first to take a flock of sheep there.
16 Terry's Royal Mail – In 1872 many of the northern mail contracts were taken over by Terry's Royal Line of Coaches. His mail runs extended north to Blinman and Sliding Rock, north-west to Port Augusta and north-east to Bimbowrie.

BLINMAN 1876

Mortlock Library: SSL:M:B360

BELTANA STATION 1876

Mortlock Library: SSL:M:B11594

day. – McClure and self jolly as sandboys. Retired to our Virtuous Couches 10.30 pm.

TUESDAY, MARCH 30 ~ Most places of business Closed all day. Bob and self went to South Blinman and had a game of Cricket in the pm. Bob astonished the Natives with his bowling and I quite astounded them, my style of play being different to anything they had before witnessed. After some scientific play, I retired gracefully for *naught* (0), adjourned to the Pub, had a few mild old Beers and returned to our Hotel for tea. About 8.30 went to the fuddle[17] did a little flirting, Bob laying it on awfully thick with a little girl about 14 years of age. Party broke up about 3.30 am. Enjoyed ourselves first Class. Got to bed a little after 4 am, awfully tired.

WEDNESDAY, MARCH 31ST /75 ~ Up at 6 am, made a start for Beltana[18] at 8 am. Bob and the Luggage by trap, self on horseback – after a very rough ride over some well-grassed Country, arrived at Bt[19] very sore and Stiff 5 pm. Brought some beer from Bl[20] for Jack Chandler[21]. Necessity Compelled

~

17 fuddle – a drink, a drunken bout.

18 Beltana – The derivation of this name appears to be incapable of definite solution. Some have said it means 'running water', another says it should be spelt Peltana meaning 'possum skin'. John Bagot said that the suffix 'ana' signified place and locality of something but was unable to say what the meaning of the prefix 'Belt' was. Moston Bive, general manager of the Beltana Pastoral Company, claimed the word was a coined one indicating the place where the station bell was rung. Beltane is an ancient celtic festival observed on May Day in Scotland and Ireland.

19 Bt – Beltana Telegraph.

20 Bl – Blinman.

21 Jack Chandler – presumably O.T. staff.

me to broach Cargo on the road, though very much against my Conscience – Went in for good old fuddle or social old Yarn. Bed 11.30 pm.

Didn't sleep much: Jack's animal Spirits elevated to an ungovernable extent – woke up about 1 am, looked in the glass and found I had Changed my Color for a more dusky one. Blyth[22] Tight as a Bottle. Had a spill from my horse on the way over – shook me up a bit.

THURSDAY, APRIL 1ST ~ Got up at 7.30 am and went to a waterhole about a mile from the Station[23], had a Bathe and returned to Breakfast:

Loafing about till Dinner time, made a good old feed (guts, as a particular friend of mine one time remarked, the reader Can refer to Mr. Lumbers for an explanation). Almost forget what roast Beef is like and shall soon be ashamed to look even an old Ram in the face. Blyth and I went over to the Nigger Camp and had a yabber. Any quantity of Royal Blood[24] to be seen and admired. Nothing doing. Like the Country first Class, most awfully hot. Bed 11.

FRIDAY, APRIL 2ND ~ Didn't get up before the lark this morning! Breakfasted about 9.15 after doing a nobbler of rum. Took Charge of the Bt office. Jack and Bob intended going to the Sliding Rock[25]. Found the responsibility weighed very heavily upon me. Required several pulls at the Monkey[26] to make me feel equal to the occasion. Lolling about all day, weather dull, o'cast – No niggers about today. Paddy Blyth and I inspected the old Bt office and outbuildings – not at all to my August Satisfaction.

Skinner[27] started from SA by the 4.30 train, don't envy him the trip atall [sic]. Tumbled into my Blue Blankets 11.30. "Its funny when you feel etc . . ."

SATURDAY, APRIL 3RD, 1875 ~ Up 8.30, feel gay as a Buck, this Country agrees with my delicate Constitution – Paddy initiated me into the secret of washing. I managed to take a little of the Color out of one of my shirts but the dirt seemed to laugh at my efforts. Spose practice will make perfect. Nothing doing.

About 8 pm half a dozen bottles of PB[28] arrived from Sliding Rock. We tested its quality and approved of it.

All retired perfectly
Sober of Course.
Karnt [sic] say at
What time.

~

22 Paddy Blyth – presumably O.T. staff.
23 the Station – Beltana Telegraph Station.
24 Royal Blood – F.J.G. being facetious about the Aborigines.
25 Sliding Rock – No mine in the Flinders showed finer prospects when first opened than did Sliding Rock, discovered in January 1870 by John Holding and Joseph Hele. A shanty settlement soon began to spring up around the mine, and in December 1872 the Government laid out a township, naming it Cadnie, an aboriginal word meaning 'rock', but the old name stuck.
26 pulls at the Monkey – probably equivalent to 'hairs of the dog'.
27 Skinner – probably Joseph Skinner, Post and Telegraph Officer at Alice Springs 1887–1892.
28 PB – Pale Brandy.

SUNDAY, APRIL 4TH ~ Turned out 8 am. Breakfast Chops and Tomata [sic] sauce a la Pickwick[29]. Wrote several Letters to my old Chinas[30]. 1 pm dinner. About 2.30 Paddy and I strolled over to the Station about 2 miles away & Saw some very fine horses and any quantity of Niggers, returned with an Appetite like an Elephant. Jack started for Bl about 12.

Turned in 8.30.

MONDAY, APRIL 5TH ~ 7.30 am Oh ye gods and very interesting Little fishes. I feel seedy. How Can this be accounted for? Echo answers how! Has the dead Marine[31] by my bedside aught to do with it? Bob's artillery[32] in Full play today. Begin to think it necessary to dock his allowance of Pea Soup. For the first time saw Camel ridden by two Affghans [sic]. It did not appear to me to be a very Comfortable mode of travelling. Chandler at Bl. Had a yarn to Chris[33] who felt seedy as usual after a trip to the Country. All hands right as a pie. Retired Gracefully 10. Kart [sic] Horse lying down all day. The Lazy Devil wouldn't do a stroke of work and I couldn't Convince him that he was loafing on Her Majesty's Govt.

TUESDAY, APRIL 6TH, 1875 ~ Up Early, went for a constitutional round the Office Building. Felt much inwiggerated!! [sic] Adelaide Mail arrived last night. Received Letters from Chris and an interesting friend. Jack[34] and Joe[35] still at Bl. Attending to office all day, very much overworked. Bob becoming quite incorrigible, has turned teetotaller, for this, I feel thankful. Haven't seen a solitary Nigger for a devil of a Time. No very exciting event to note except that I managed to knock over a Crow at about 5 yards distance. Wrote to D[36].

WEDNESDAY, APRIL 7TH ~ 8.30 aroused from my Slumbers by a very small fly who was feasting on the delicate tip of my Proboscis. After Breakfast and sending in the Reports, settled down quietly on Jack's Couch which by the way is not quite as soft as I should like. Jack and Joe arrived about 4.30, Much disappointed through not getting my Beer.
Repaired to my virtuous Couch at 9.

THURSDAY, APRIL 8TH, 1875 ~ Turned out 8.30, Awfully seedy, too much Medical Comforts last night. Was frightened nearly out of my Life by a Nigger who Came behind me & in a deep gutteral [sic] voice, said, "Waugh". I was lying down under some bushes in a Creek about 100 Yards from the Stn at the time – to make matters look worse he had a spear & was quietly leaning on it when I turned round. Paddy and self spent our afternoon washing. Managed to wash about

~

29 a la Pickwick – from *The Pickwick Papers*, first novel of Charles Dickens. The story is of the adventures of Mr Pickwick and his friends who go on a journey of observation of men and manners. F.J.G. obviously appreciated Dickens's *Pickwick Papers* and the spellings here, and in several other places, are deliberate. Dickens was probably the best known, most widely read, author of the era and, indeed, was prescribed reading in schools for the better part of the next century.
30 Chinas – rhyming slang, china plate = mate.
31 dead Marine – an empty bottle.
32 artillery – flatulence.
33 Chris – presumably O.T. staff.
34 Jack – Jack Chandler.
35 Joe – Joseph Skinner.
36 D – unknown, perhaps 'an interesting friend' whose letter arrived on the same day.

two dozen & half[37] between us, Got my Knuckles Chipped and have resolved not to do anymore of such artistic work unless Compelled to do so by force of Circumstances.

Retired Gracefully 9.30.

FRIDAY, APRIL 9TH, 1875 ~ Turned out 8.30, gay as a buck. Any quantity of Niggers about today just when they were not wanted. My hands very sore, the Effects of yesterday afternoon's work, must have used too much Soda. Wrote Home, also Chris and Clark. Had about 20 drops of rain during the Evening. Good allowance for this Country, if we had too much the people would make beasts of themselves. 10 pm, Jack and I paid the Nigger's Camp a visit, found several of the sable Darkies tight. Bunked in on the floor, 10.50 pm.

SATURDAY, APRIL 10TH, 75 ~ Roused out at 8.30 am.

Loafing about all morning. 1 pm Went in for a Good feed of Mutton. All hands astonished at the Storage Capacity of my hold –

Making preparations for our Start on Monday, had a very Good hint that we were to be sumptiously [sic] entertained at a Supper of Pea Soup before leaving – Shall take every Care not to sleep within 20 yards of my Virtuous Friend Bob for the next two days after the Pea Soup fuddle. The Blue Blankets very Kindly recd [sic] my valuable Carcase at 10 Precisely.

SUNDAY, APRIL 11, 1875 ~ Turned out about 9.30. Nothing doing all day. All hands jolly and looking forward to our Start tomorrow. Bob's artillery again in full play – Pea Soup

Dinner. Good old Snooze in the PM. Spent the Evening aboosing [sic] our Neighbours and smoking Govt Tobacco. Bed 10.30.

MONDAY, APRIL 12TH ~ Up at 7.30, Put all our Luggage on the Waggon [sic]. 11.30 Bob started with the Wagon. Joe and I obliged to stay behind as our Horses Could not be found. Missed Bob's Company from the festive Board. 5 Gallons Beer arrived from Bl two hours too late to go by Wagon. Paddy Blyth and I went to the Station in the Evening, visited Govt. House[38] where we had some rum which Considerably upset Pat's Equilibrium, returned to Stn about 10 and pitched into the Beer. Paddy Got awfully tight.

Got to Bed 11.30.

TUESDAY, APRIL 13TH ~ Turned out 8 – when I awoke found Poor old Pat huddled up all of a heap on the floor. Poor Devil looked like a Biled Owl. Horses turned up about 10.30 AM. After Cracking several Bottles and stowing away two in my Swag, Joe and I started, expected to meet the Party at Windy Creek, when we got there found to our disgust that they had gone on – Caught them at Leigh's Creek[39], a distance

~

37 two dozen & half – items of clothing.

38 Govt. House – station homestead.

39 Leigh's Creek – The first white man to see the creek was Edward John Eyre, who crossed it on his way north in 1840 but didn't name it. It was named after Harry Leigh, the first stockman of Alexander Glen, who took up this part of the country and stocked it with cattle in 1856. A coal deposit was discovered in 1885 and is still being mined to generate electricity for South Australia.

of 25 miles from Beltana. There is a plentiful supply of water here. Was shown the Grave of a girl [?] who had Committed Suicide. Slept underneath Nature's Canopy for the first time.

WEDNESDAY, APRIL 14TH ~ Turned out 7. Slept like a top during the Night felt very much refreshed. 9 AM, Jack the Cook and I started for the Myrtle Station[40] 13 miles from our Camp. Purchased a sheep, Killed him and packed a half each on our Saddles and returned to Camp at 6 PM. Saw some fine Niggers at the Myrtle. Had a good feed of salt Horse for Dinner. Country very dry and water very salt. Spent the Evening spinning Cuffers[41] round the Camp fire. Shall have to Camp here 3 or 4 days to salt sheep. Turned in 9 pm.

THURSDAY, APRIL 15TH, 1875 ~ Roused out 7 am. Camping out makes me rise Early. Still Camped on Leigh's Creek. Nothing doing all morning. In the PM had a game of Pitch and Toss. We have two Cooks in our party, Jack Howie and a Nigger named Fergusson who swears he's a Scotchman. They appear to be jealous of each other and it is great fun to listen to them Jawing. Got some Sheep. My Knife tasted Blood for the first time. Had some Songs and music during the Evening.

FRIDAY, APRIL 16TH, 1875 ~ Turned out 8 AM. Fine day. Men salting Sheep and getting everything ready for a Start tomorrow. Getting quite used to Camping out and find it is a deal more comfortable in a Civilized habitation. Millions of flies about and find them awfully Troublesome. They appear to be a different species to the Common fly seen about Adelaide, but are far more troublesome. Bob and I laid it out in the waggon all day improving our minds by reading, smoking etc. Got to Bed about 9.

SATURDAY, APRIL 17TH ~ Up at 6.30, very Cold strong wind blowing. Had Breakfast and made a start about 8.30. Crossed Glen's Gums and Camped about 12 or 13 miles from Leigh's Creek. Rode in waggon, Skinner and Bob on Horseback. We are Camped on the Great Western Plain and are obliged to send our Horses 4 or 5 miles to water, very little feed about except Saltbush. Roads rather Bad – Nothing in the shape of timber visible from our Camp except small teatree Bushes. Appetite something tremendous. Bob Ill with Measles. Turned in 8 – raining a little.

SUNDAY, APRIL 18TH, 1875 ~ Turned out 6.30 AM. Had some rain during the night. Horses Got in and made a start about 8.30. Bob in wagon, Joe and I on Horseback – had a few showers during the morning. Made a halt at the Red Hill and had a little bread and meat – No Grass whatever along road. Camped at St. A'Becketts[42], Dr. Brown's[43] Stn,

~

40 Myrtle Station – Myrtle Springs Station.

41 Cuffers – off the cuff information, 'yarns'.

42 St. A'Becketts – a waterhole (which has now silted up completely) near Lake Torrens. Named by Samuel Parry on August 10, 1858, after Archbishop A'Beckett. The name was unofficially corrupted to Sandy Bagot Ponds.

43 Dr. Brown – This would be Browne – William James and John Harris – both medical practitioners who became pastoralists and at one time owned fifteen large stations.

where we met Mr. Ernest Giles[44], the Explorer, who had penetrated 350 Miles inland from Fowler's Bay. All his horses had died thro [sic] want of water and for 8 days, while travelling 220 miles, the Camels were without water.

Measles fairly out on Bob, he looks very like a Boiled Lobster – Obliged to rig up our tarpaulins on account of the rain – Our present Camp about 18 miles from last night's resting places. White women becoming very scarce, only seen one since leaving Beltana. We have to console ourselves by looking over the leaves of an old Volume of The Bow Bells[45]. Like travelling A1. In the Evening Joe and I visited Mr. Giles' Camp and spent a Couple of hours there, of Course he acknowledged our superior Knowledge on Exploring Matters. Turned in 8.30 pm.

MONDAY, APRIL 19TH, 1875 ~ Turned out 7. Very little rain during the night. Slept A1 underneath the tarpaulin. Men had some difficulty in finding horses so did not make a start till 10 AM. Horses jibbed like mad – a Case of all hands at the wheel. Passed a Mob of Cattle, about 400, in Charge of Mr. Harry Gosse[46], en route for West of the Peake[47]. Still travelling on the Western Plain. Camped at The Govt. Gums[48], 10 miles from St. A'Becketts, where I met an old friend of Mine – Mr. Kent who was in Charge of a Hawker's Cart. Threatening rain all day. Pitched our Tarpaulin. Very Good water in the Govt. well here, the first decent drink since leaving Blinman. Explored the ruins of the old

Telegraph Station at one time under the *Management* of the Notorious Mr. Bell. Bless his old Gums. Purchased a Monkey Jacket[49] and a Pocket Knife from Kent. The Members of the Expedition opened their hearts and purchased two penny whistles. Wasteful Extravagance, oh My Eye. Bob progressing favorably. After a very big Man Yabber turned in about 10.

God Save The Queen.

TUESDAY, APRIL 20, 1875 ~ Turned out 7.30. Had been dewing heavily during the night. Everything uncomfortably damp. Lolled about all morning. Could not make an early start as there is no water for the next 35 miles – Packed up and made a start at 3.15 PM, travelled over a Portion of

~

44 Mr. Ernest Giles (1835–1897). Born Bristol, migrated in 1850 to Adelaide. Joined Victorian goldrush in 1852, subsequently led a roaming life in the outback, taking part in several minor expeditions seeking new pastures beyond the Darling River. Late in 1875, he set out from Beltana on his third major expedition and, by following the Aborigines' well system, crossed the Great Victoria Desert to reach Western Australia on 4 November.

45 The Bow Bells – a weekly magazine of general literature November 1862 to March 1897.

46 Mr. Harry Gosse (1848–1888). Born in London and came to Adelaide with his family in 1851. He worked on the construction of the Overland Telegraph Line. With his brother William, he went exploring in 1873–1874 to look for a passage between the O.T.L. and Perth. This was the expedition which discovered and named Ayers Rock.

47 Peake – named by Stuart after Edward J. Peake, son-in-law of one of the explorer's patrons, James Chambers.

48 Govt. Gums – name has been changed to Farina.

49 Monkey Jacket – a close fitting short jacket 'with no more tail than a monkey'.

Lake Eyre[50], very boggy, Waggon horses jibbed like blazes. Passed a most peculiar water worn mound, which we named "Bully's Nob". Passed the Grave of some Poor fellow who was found dead. Camped on a sandhill about 14 miles from the Gums. Feed tolerably Good. Turned in about 9.30.

WEDNESDAY, APRIL 21ST, 1875 ~ Turned out about 5.30, had breakfast and started for the Booloo Springs[51], a 20 Mile stage – at 6.30. Camped at 11 for lunch, having found some water for the Horses in some Crab holes[52]. Saw the Grave of a Man who was found dead by one of our party about 3 months since. Got in our Arab Steeds and made a fresh start at 1.15. Waggon Horses stuck us up in a little sand and detained us 2 hours. Found some water in some mud holes and Camped at 5.30, having travelled about 18 miles. Turned in 8.00. Slung My hammock to the Shafts of the waggon.

THUSDAY, APRIL 22ND, 1875 ~ Turned out 7.00. Had a Devil of a job to Catch my Horse – Barry and Joe galloping after him for half an hour. Made a start about 9 AM. Getting into the hilly Country again. Crossed the Booloo Creek and passed the Booloo Springs. These springs – 3 in number – come from solid rock, any quantity of Water but very bitter and salt. Passed thro' some pretty Country and camped on the Dwyndie Creek, having travelled 8 miles! Big journey for one day. Water on the flat in Mud Holes – Creek quite dry. Saw a natural Pan in a large rock where there was a good supply of rain water – quite a treat. Bed 8.30

ERNEST GILES

Mortlock Library: SSL:M:B8501

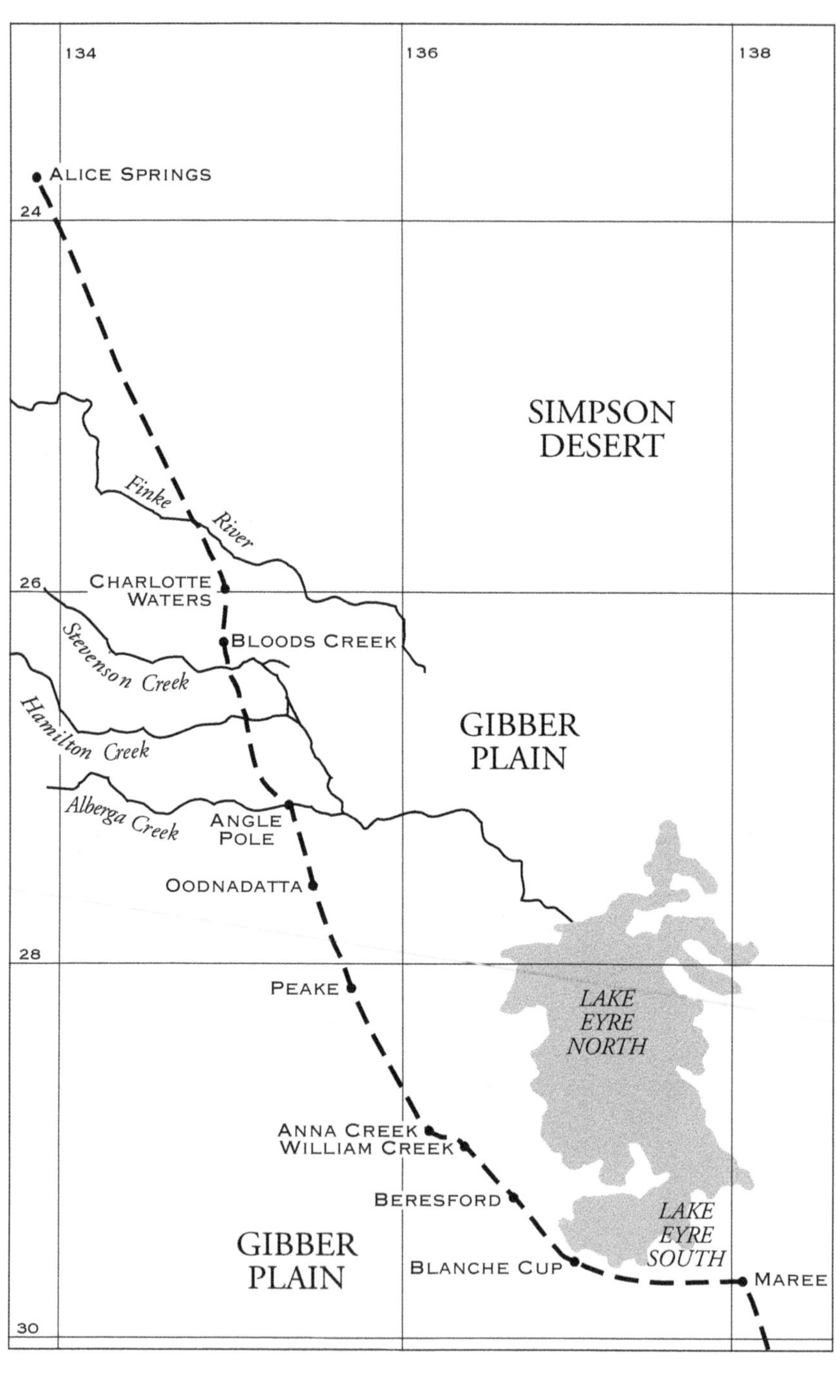

134
136
138
ALICE SPRINGS
24
SIMPSON DESERT
Finke River
26
CHARLOTTE WATERS
BLOODS CREEK
Stevenson Creek
Hamilton Creek
GIBBER PLAIN
Alberga Creek
ANGLE POLE
OODNADATTA
28
PEAKE
LAKE EYRE NORTH
ANNA CREEK
WILLIAM CREEK
BERESFORD
LAKE EYRE SOUTH
GIBBER PLAIN
BLANCHE CUP
MAREE
30

FRIDAY, APRIL 23RD, 1875 ~ Turned out about 7. Between 6 and 700 head of Cattle Camped 50 yards from our Camp all night, Kicking up a Devil of a row of Course. We are to be met at the Welcome[53] today with fresh Horses. Our present team of warmed-up Skeletons are to have a spell – It is a great tax on their strength driving them such long stages as 8 Miles a day. Made a start 10 AM. Heard at Collano [Callana] Station, no feed at Welcome, so Camped in some good feed about 6 miles from last night's Camp. Saw a few Niggers at Collano both sexes being in full dress with an old Shirt or waistband – My Modesty received a sad shock. My friend Bob seemed to Admire a young Lubra[54] named Nellie, a member of the "Dyerie"[55] tribe of Natives – Must admit she had a Glossy black skin and a Tolerably good set of Ivorys. Flies something dreadful. Could keep half a dozen little Nigger Boys engaged brushing them away while we eat a

~

50 Lake Eyre – The world's fifth largest terminal lake, is the geodetic sump of the largest internal drainage system in the world. The lake is situated in the most arid part of the country with a mean annual rainfall of less than 125 mm, and an annual evaporation rate of about 2.5 metres (Bonython, 1955). Lake Eyre is coincident with the lowest part of the Australian continent. The Lake was named after Edward John Eyre, who was born in 1815 at Whipsnade, England.

51 Booloo Springs – Booloo is an Aboriginal word for 'white'.

52 Crab holes – These are holes of varying depth (from 30 cm to 1 metre), the smallest of them wide enough to admit the foot of a horse.

53 Welcome – Welcome Springs, Aboriginal name is Callana.

54 Lubra – A Tasmanian Aboriginal name for a woman, introduced first into Victoria by Tasmanian settlers.

55 Dyerie = Dieri.

bit of Scram[56]. Had a juvenile snooze in the afternoon.

Our Band favoured us with a Choice selection of Operatic Music during the Evening. I may mention that "Old Dog Tray" "Dixie's Land"[57] and other famous pieces were performed.

Turned in about 9.

God Save the Queen.

SATURDAY, APRIL 24TH, 1875 ~ Flooded out at 1.40 AM, raining heavily, all hands obliged to take refuge in the Wagon – Bedding wet. After rain ceased made a fire and dried ourselves. Roads too sticky to start today. Day seemed very long. Man from Strangways[58] met us with two fine Horses.

Turned in about 9.

Bob Ill again.

SUNDAY, APRIL 25TH, 1875 ~ Turned out 7 am. Very heavy dew falling all night. Had Breakfast and made a start at 9.30. Crossed the Welcome Creek, in the bed of which are several fine springs. The water tastes very much of Gunpowder but is not unpleasant to drink. Passed a Grave Covered with stones. Crossed Wanganya Creek[59], travelled through some hilly Country and Camped on Paull's Creek, a distance of 16 Miles from last night's Camp: Any quantity of Gum Trees here. Bob still very unwell. The Strangways Horses have proved a great acquisition to our party. They are worth the whole of our old Skrews. Had a smart Shower just before Sundown. Luckily we had our tent rigged up.

Turned in 8.15.

MONDAY, APRIL 26TH, 1875 ~ Turned out 7 am. Blowing Great Guns all night but no rain. Tobacco day today. We are allowed 1 lb. Per Month. Packed up and made a start about 8.30. Travelled through hilly Country. Arrived at The Finniss Cattle Station[60] just in time to have a good old feed of Salt Horse – quite a luxury after living on Mutton so long. We purchased 25 lbs. of Beef. At the present moment we are stuck up Crossing the Finniss Sandhills. Our team Consists of 6 horses, 4 of which are not worth the Swearing they Cause. We have all had a turn at the wheel but it's no go, the wretches won't budge an inch. It is now 4 o'clock. God Knows when we shall get out of this fix. 5 PM, All hands being quite exhausted with their efforts and Horses still refuse duty, have struck Camp. Skinner and I went back to the Station in the Evening and arranged with Mr. Harry Gosse to help us out of the Mire. Rigged my Hammock on the Shafts and turned in about 8.30. Bob still unwell. Ye Gods and juvenile fishes!

~

56 Scram – normally 'scran' – food.

57 Dixie's Land – well-known American song of the time.

58 Strangways – Strangways Springs, named after Henry Bull Templar Strangways, who outlived all the other members of the first 'Parliament under Responsible Government'. He was Premier once, Attorney-General twice and Commissioner of Crown Lands four times.

59 Wanganya Creek – now known as Wangianna, Aboriginal for 'hill of the plain'.

60 Finnis Cattle Station – named after Colonel Boyle Travers Finniss. His public offices in South Australia were legion. He came to South Australia as Assistant Surveyor to Colonel Light and successively filled the positions of Deputy Surveyor General, Commissioner of Police and Police Magistrate, Colonial Treasurer and Registrar General and Colonial Secretary.

TUESDAY, APRIL 27TH, 1875 ~ Turned out 7.30. Made a start about 12.30 and with the assistance of Gosse's Horses got through the worst part of the Sandhills. Pitched Camp about 3.30 having travelled between 3 & 4 Miles – Nothing very startling to note. Gosse visited our Camp in the Evening and we smoked several and seveereal [sic] pipes of good old Bacca. Bob getting round again. Turned in about 9.30.

WEDNESDAY, APRIL 28TH, 1875 ~ From my Virtuous Couch I arose at 7. Made a start about 9 and our Blood stock showed their Mettle by getting bogged on the first little sandhill. Had to draw on Gosse's Good nature again. Crossed the Gregory Creek[61] and passed through some useless Country Covered with small Ironstone pebbles. Camped about a mile from the "Dyntna Dyntna Springs"[62]. Expect we shall experience some difficulty in getting up the Yedney Creek[63] tomorrow. (This is a Creek which I believe has been frequently navigated by old Cart Horse). Saw several dead Marines along the road side. Our Darkie Cook says they have done their duty once and are ready to do it again. Hot discussion between the Rival Cook's Towser and Snowy during the Evening. Old Towser is a ripper at Spinning a Cuffer, licks me into a Cocked Hat. The Leader of this Great Expedition, and a man, start for the Strangways tomorrow morning to arrange about Horses meeting us from the Peake.

Not atall [sic] OK. Turned in 7.30.

THURSDAY, APRIL 29TH, 1875 ~ Roused out at 7. All hands Complain that I've been snoring like the very devil all night. Surely this is a mistake. Skinner and Man started about 8.30, Party at 9.30. Had to unload Wagon Crossing the Priscilla Sandhill[64] and hump the things for about 100 yards over the Hill. Horses rec'd the blessings of all hands and took it very Christian-like, not even pricking up their Ears. Any quantity of water on the table lands. Struck work about 2 pm having Carted ourselves about 10 miles. Done a festive old talk during evening, principal subject of Conversation, Tom Sayers, Jack Heenan and others. Turned in about 9.

FRIDAY, APRIL 30TH, 1875 ~ Turned out 7 am. Dug a hole about 4 x 4, 2 feet deep and named it "The Pickwick Panikan". Started at 8.30. Crossed Stuart's Creek[65] where I saw a large Black Snake and hundreds of ducks. There is a fine,

~

61 Gregory Creek – named by P.E. Warburton in 1858, after Augustus Charles Gregory. Gregory left Moreton Bay in Queensland on 24 March, 1858 to follow the tracks of the explorer Leichhardt who, on his expedition ten years previously, had disappeared with his party into the Interior.

62 Dyntna Dyntna Springs – presumably local Aboriginal name. It is an example of a mound spring. Mound springs are small but important sources of permanent water extending along an arc throughout north-east South Australia. All of these springs have Aboriginal names and particular mythological associations. Gillen and his friends were cutting fairly obviously across a landscape redolent with meaning for Aboriginal people; he was to gain an appreciation of this within a few years, in sharp distinction to most of the white population of the centre.

63 Yedney Creek – presumably local Aboriginal name.

64 Priscilla Sandhill – named by explorer John McDouall Stuart after Miss Priscilla Chambers, who became Mrs. Bickford. She arrived in Adelaide in 1837 when she was eighteen. She is said to have tied herself to the mast of the ship to experience, on deck, a storm it was weathering.

65 Stuart's Creek – named by B.H. Babbage after John McDouall Stuart (who changed the name to Chambers Creek out of gratitude to one of his patrons, James Chambers. However, Babbage's will has endured.)

large and deep pool of permanent water up the Creek about 100 yards from the Crossing: Great pity we have no Gun with us. Camped on the Bombombie Creek[66] about 11 miles from last night's Camp – Just as we were about to retire gracefully, it commenced to rain. All hands bundled into the waggon till the shower passed. Slept on the Shafts. Light showers occasionally.

SATURDAY, MAY 1ST, 75 ~ Turned out 6.30, slight showers all night. Started at 9 AM. Passed some Springs on the Top of Two hard Limestone hills, name unknown. Water tastes of Soda – Called in at Mt. Hamilton Station. The dwelling house is built on the side of a little hill, on the top of which there is a fine spring of water coming from the solid rock. Most of the Springs in the North West are similarly situated. Camped on Mt. Hamilton Creek[67] where we saw any quantity of ducks. Weather threatening so pitched our tent.

All hands turned in about 8.30.

SUNDAY, MAY 2ND ~ Spelled all day as there is plenty feed and water for Horses. Our Dog suffering from the effects of strychnine, gave him a good dose of Salt and he is now fast recovering. Mailman Called at Camp, received a letter from D, also parcel from Clark. Done a little washing in the morning. Amused ourselves reading. Day seemed awfully long.

Turned in 7.30.

P.S. I always keep good hours.

MONDAY, MAY 3RD, 1875 ~ Arose from my virtuous Couch about 6.30. Had Breakfast and started at 9 AM. Crossed Mt. Hamilton Creek. Saw the Graves of some Niggers who had recently died of the Measles. Had a look at "Blanche Cup"[68], a very fine spring of water on the top of a small Limestone Hill about 30 feet above the Level of the surrounding Country. This natural Cup is evidently the result of a volcanic eruption at some remote date. Some Bushmen say it has never yet been bottomed. There are at least a dozen springs on a square mile between The Cup and The Kewson. No trees whatever to be seen except in the Creeks. Travelled about 12 miles and Camped a couple of Miles South of the Kewson Springs. Arrived at Camp about 1. After dinner, wrote three letters.

Had some music after tea and turned in about 8.30.

TUESDAY, MAY 4TH ~ Roused out 7 AM, fresh as a lark. Filled my hold and made a start about 9 AM. Crossed the Kewson Creek, passed Kewson Springs on the right, travelled through some hilly Country and camped about 1/2 mile North

~

66 Bombombie Creek – presumably local Aboriginal name.

67 Mt. Hamilton Creek – George Hamilton, Commissioner of Police who must have been in the good books of the explorers, because Eyre, McKinlay and Warburton kept him in mind when filling the map. He founded the Adelaide Club, where he died in 1883 following a seizure after taking part in ceremony connected with the opening of Parliament.

68 Blanche Cup – a 12-metre-high, sugar-loaf hill with a strongly flowing spring on top and a hot water spring alongside. Named after Blanche, daughter of Francis Skurray, wife of Governor MacDonnell, this is another example of a mound spring.

of the Beresford Hill[69] and Warburtons Springs[70]. Mosquitos becoming troublesome, shall soon have to use our Nets. My Horse's back sore, gave him a spell and rode in the Wagon. Sat round the Camp fire after tea and abused our neighbors [sic].

WEDNESDAY, MAY 5TH, 1875 ~ Got up about 7. Had Breakfast and made a start about 8.30. Horse's back still sore, rode in Wagon. Arrived at the Strangways Springs Station about 1, just in time for dinner. Met Harry Gosse here, the Messrs Hogarth[71] jolly, fine fellows. Rec'd a Letter from home and was glad to hear all well and jolly. Strangways Springs Station is built on a long range, this range is Covered with Springs. Water beastly. Had some songs and Music during the evening. Lord Poop[72] has sadly degenerated since leaving Adelaide. Gave him my humble advice. We are staying at Govt. House. Turned in (To Bed) about 11, Perfectly Sober.

THURSDAY, MAY 6TH, 1875 ~ Pulled out of Bed at 8 AM very much against my will. Had breakfast. Water giving me particular blazes, pains in my stumjack [sic] nearly all day. Bowels going off their Chump altogether. Exchanged some of my Books with Lord Poop, whom I have re-christened Ramisses [sic] the 2nd. All the Shepherds employed on this Station are Niggers, they seem to answer the purpose equally as well as white men – It is not atall uncommon for one Sable Darkie to have 2 or 3 Wives. Fine looking young half-caste here. 'Spose it's a Chip off some old Block. Expect to make a start tomorrow. Got our Clothes washed by a Negress. Any quantity of wild dogs about this district.

FRIDAY, MAY 7TH, 1875 ~ Turned out at 8 AM – Bad night's rest suffering from Dysentry, affects [sic] of Spring water. Think this water would Kill me in about a fortnight. Some fine Blackfellows on this Station, some of their religious observances are very Barbarous – For instance when a Male Native of the tribe reaches the age of 18 or 20, he is tied down and the Medicine Man of the tribe slits the tube of the Penis from the top to the root[73]. It is a known fact that very few of the Natives have large families – Reading most of the day. Detained here for supply of Meat. Men Gone out to bring in Cattle.

SATURDAY, MAY 8TH, 1875 ~ Scarcely any sleep last night. This water still giving me fits. Have taken doses of Cholera Drops[74] and Chlorydyne[75] but they don't take desired affect [sic]. Reading all the morning. After Dinner took 6 Holloways

~

69 Beresford Hill – named after G.W.D. Beresford, Private Secretary to Governor MacDonnell.
70 Warburtons Springs – named after Peter Egerton Warburton (1813–1889). Born Cheshire, England. He arrived in Adelaide to take up appointment as Police Commissioner, December 1853. In 1858 he explored country lying west of Lake Torrens and proved that Lake Torrens and Lake Eyre were separate entities.
71 Messrs Hogarth – Thomas, legislator and pioneer pastoralist, and his brother John, arrived at South Arm in the ship *Delhi* on 21 December, 1839.
72 Lord Poop – unidentified, but clearly one of F.J.G.'s travelling companions. Possibly Bob, who had difficulties after dining on pea-soup.
73 Gillen was to make an extensive study of this initiatory rite, which was later written up in subsequent publications. For a recent detailed discussion of the practice and mythology see Cawte et al.
74 Cholera Drops – conventional medicinal aid for the era.
75 Chlorodyne – tincture of chloroform and morphine used to treat diarrhoea.

Pills[76], feel they are doing me Good. God Bless Professor Holloways old Gums. Much Better in Evening – appetite returning – Skinner's eating Capabilities getting very great. Cattle Got in and a Bullock killed. Shall have some fresh Beef tomorrow.

SUNDAY, MAY 9TH, 1875 ~ Turned out about 8, feel first Class this morning, thanks to Holloways Bullets. Had some Steak for Breakfast, by jingo it did go down properly. Reading all day. We start tomorrow and expect to reach the Peake in 9 days. My Horse from here is, I believe, a regular tartar.

MONDAY, MAY 10TH, 1875 ~ Packed up our Swags, had breakfast and made a Start about 10.30. My Horse a brute, had some trouble to mount him. Travelled through about 5 miles of Sandhills. Barry and I here got off our Horses to wait for the waggon. When it Came up I mounted again but was soon put down on terra firma – my neck sadly in danger – Horses stuck us up in the sand about 6 Miles from the Stn. – obliged to let them go after making every effort to make them go. Had to send 1,1/2 miles for water.

Turned in about 8.30.

TUESDAY, MAY 11TH ~ Turned out about 7. Had a Couple of light showers after Breakfast. Got Horses in about 10, but Could not get them to pull atall, after exhausting ourselves with pushing the waggon, took half the load off, after this they made a start and took the things to the Yellow waterhole. Driver returned to Camp for remainder of Cargo – Rode my fiery Charger, did not feel atal [sic] Comfortable on his back. Camped at the Yellow waterhole having travelled about 1,1/2 miles!

This is one of the longest day's journey on record. Blowing Great Guns all day. In the evening we were honored by a visit from a Peake Nigger – a most ugly specimen of Human Nature. He is called Ourang Outang by the Whites and takes to the characteristic name Kindly. His native name is "Obijie". Another horse arrived for us, hope with this addition to be able to push on quickly.

Collected a lot of different Grasses and pressed them.

Tumbled into the Blankets about 8.30.

Wednesday, May 12th, 1875 ~ Got up about 7 – morning very Cold. Made a start about 8.30. Cameron[77] riding my Charger. Horses stuck us up at the first Sandhill. We were obliged to unload and take the things over in small quantities. Getting heartily sick of this Humbugging – Skinner started with a Man to bring the Peake Horses down as it is no use trying to get on with our present Team of frames. All my Christian fortitude and forbearance used up! Camped about 2.30. Have been 6 hours travelling over 2 Miles. Our waggon has not, at the outside, more than a ton on board. Would not mind it so much if we had some Medical Comforts to console ourselves with.

~

76 Holloways Pills – a universal remedy of the time, widely advertised.

77 Cameron – presumed O.T. staff.

THURSDAY, MAY 13TH, 1875 ~ Made a start about 9 AM. Got out of the last of Strangways Sandhills. Passed the "William" Spring[78]. Got on first class till we came to the Breakfast-time Sand. Here the Horses followed up their old rule, with a great deal of pushing and swearing managed to get through about a mile of sand. We intended making the Breakfast-time waterhole tonight, but were obliged to give up the idea through Horses jibbing. Struck Camp about 5 PM, all hands thoroughly tired! Found some water about 1/2 miles from Camp – filled all our waterbags. Day very Cold, strong wind blowing. Would give a trifle for a mild old Nip of P.B.

FRIDAY, MAY 14TH, 1875 ~ Turned out about 8, found all hands had had Breakfast – Decided to Camp here until Skinner returns with Peake Horses. After helping to cart sufficient water for the day, camped in the waggon with a Good Book and my festive old pipe. My appetite today astonishing. For dinner I consumed four doughboys[79]. Bob was pleased to Call this Gourmandizing. He does not care to be reminded that he consumed a quart of Soup, 1/4 of yard of damper and about 1/2 lb. of Salt Horse. Very mild. Expect Mailman to pass tomorrow, anxiously waiting for our Letters. 5 PM Skinner returned with a fresh team of 6 Horses, if they are as good as they look, we shall do a big journey tomorrow. Our party now Consists of 9 Men & 14 Horses. Expect to reach the Peake Tuesday night, that is if horses carry out our expectations. All hands sat round the Campfire spinning yarns till 10 pm. This is the latest hour we have kept while on the road since leaving Beltana.

Chops and Tomarto [sic] Sauce, Yures

Pickwick.

SATURDAY, MAY 15TH, 1875 ~ Turned out about 6.50, roused about 5.30 by the Black Cook who had, to all appearances, suddenly taken leave of his senses. Made a start 8.30. Peake Horses shaping first Class. Passed through some hilly Country, saw Mt. Margaret[80] in the distance. One of the Party informs me there are springs on this Mount always at a boiling heat – Crossed Sunny Creek, I named a little creek, coming from the hills on the left and emptying itself into "The Sunny", "The Sweedlepipe Creek". The name is taken from one of Dicken's Characters in "Martin Chuzzlewitt". Camped at the "London Spa"[81], a spring situated on the top of a hill, prettily surrounded by trees and different Shrubs. Water quite warm but otherwise the best spring water we have yet used. Have at last got perfect Control of my Charger – was very nearly Coming to grief while mounting him this morning, the excessive weight of my Stern will not allow me to get into

~

78 William Spring – William Creek, represents a compliment paid by John McDouall Stuart to second son of John Chambers.

79 doughboys – a rounded mass of dough boiled or steamed as a dumpling or deep-fried and served as a hot bread.

80 Mt. Margaret – named by P.E. Warburton for Margaret, wife of Arthur John Baker, Superintendent of Adelaide Fire Brigade. She was sister of Lady Ayers.

81 London Spa – Loudon Springs, discovered by Stuart on 23 June, 1859 and named after James Loudon, the manager of Mount Arden Station and founder of Yadlamalka and Cariewerloo Stations.

the saddle quickly without being Clumsy. Distance travelled about 22 Miles, so much for the Peake team. Yarning round the Camp fire until after 9.

I wonder what my old Chums in Adelaide are up to at the present moment? No doubt some of them are on the 10/- side of Rundle Street[82].

SUNDAY, MAY 16TH, 1875 ~ Turned out about 7.30. Started 9 AM. My Charger rather frisky today. Travelled 9 miles, Camped at Umbum[83], Bagot's old Stn – there are a few old Huts here, we took possession of one for Cooking purposes, wood awfully scarce – There is a fine hole full of water here, we tried to Catch some fish but didn't even get a solitary nibble for our trouble – Met a Nigger here who minds the mail horses and rejoices in the name of Dick – He is a most Comical old Beggar and is blessed with two wives. Find the hut very Convenient, there is a table and some forms inside. Went in for a little Gymnastics.

MONDAY, MAY 17TH, 1875 ~ Turned out 6.30. Rigged my Hammock on the Shafts last night, slept awfully Cold. Started for the Bulldog Creek at 8.35. Travelled through some irregular Country, in some places where the ground was bare of vegetation there was a Coating of soda[84] about an eighth of an inch thick. Distance travelled 22 miles – this is something like travelling. Skinner suffering from the Mumps. Bob and I start early tomorrow morning on horseback and expect to reach the Peake about 12.

Retired Gracefully at 9.

TUESDAY, MAY 18TH, 1875 ~ Turned out about 6.30, had breakfast and made a start about 8.25. Arrived at the Peake about 12. Here we had the pleasure of again seeing a white woman, in the Person of Mrs. Blood[85]. We did not require much penetration to notice that the magic hands of a woman had been used about the house, everything seemed so very different to what we have been used to lately. There are dozens of Niggers about here, very few of them possess the luxury of an article of Clothing. The females of the tribe have one of the front teeth knocked out and both sexes are tatooed [sic], in some cases, hideously so. We are going to have a good look at some of them tomorrow. The Peake station is built on the Freeling Springs[86] and is surrounded by hills. Oh, bye the bye [sic], I have quite an exciting event to note – I was taken for Mueller[87] by Mrs. Blood!! Skinner, Bob and I are trying to

~

82 10/- side of Rundle Street – possibly refers to the northern side of Rundle Street where the more prosperous shops were.
83 Umbum – owned by J. and E.M. Bagot and formerly called Mt Margaret Station. Edward Meade Bagot was born on 13 December, 1822 at Rockforest, County Clare, Ireland, the third son of Captain Charles Harvey Bagot. He arrived in South Australia in 1840 and quickly became a successful pastoralist. In 1870 Bagot won a contract for constructing a portion of the Overland Telegraph Line which he completed on time.
84 Coating of soda – a white powdery coating. The springs and low-lying claypans in the vicinity of Lake Eyre deposit salts and other minerals, eg. gypsum.
85 Mrs. Blood – wife of man after whom Blood's Creek is named.
86 Freeling Springs – named after Major General Sir Arthur Henry Freeling. In January 1849, soon after his marriage to a daughter of the late Sir A. Rivers Bart, he came to South Australia and was appointed Surveyor General and Colonial Engineer, as successor to Colonel Frome.
87 Johannes Ferdinand Mueller (1853–1922) was the first station master at Alice Springs and served from early January 1872 to 31 August, 1879. He then worked in South Australia before leaving the Post and Telegraph Department in 1884.

MEN AT BLANCHE CUP 1889

Mortlock Library: SSL:M:B13358

PEAKE TELEGRAPH STATION 1872

Mortlock Library: SSL:M:B11364

get Mr. Todd's permission to go ahead of the Party – if the permission is Granted we shall reach the Alice within a month. Blood opened a bottle of PB in the evening and we did our best to make a hole in it. Mueller and Tucker are expected here tomorrow.

Turned in at the ungodly hour of 11.50.

WEDNESDAY, MAY 19TH, 1875 ~ Turned out about 8 AM. Slept in the office, Bob again Complaining of my snoring – must really take some steps to remedy this disagreeable Evil. Mr. Todd consented to our going ahead. All very glad to get away from the Waggon. Any number of juvenile niggers about today – there are at least 20 and all perfectly naked. The young devils look like a lot of Monkeys scampering about. They live principally on Snakes, Lizards and herbage and all look in excellent Condition. Had a mild old Second Mate's Nobler[88] [sic] at 11. Truly I have a great respect for our worthy mayor. Mueller, Tucker and party arrived about 4.30. Tucker is a rum little Devil. PB flying about in all directions during the evening, two or three of the Lightning Squirters[89] got off their Chump[90] a little. Finished up at Bagot's Government House[91], where we had some PB served out most sumptiously [sic] from a tin jug.

Turned in about 11.50.

~

88 Second Mate's Nobbler – a short drink, a fluid ounce.

89 Lightning Squirters – telegraph operators.

90 off their Chump – angry, or boisterously loud and silly.

91 Bagot's Government House – Bagot's main homestead. The tin jug means they were in the dining room and that they were welcome visitors.

THURSDAY, MAY 20TH, 1875 ~ Turned out about 8, felt rather hot in the lower regions. Mueller very dicky, Tucker suffering from headache – Poor devils. Made all preparations for a start tomorrow. This place literally stinks of lightning. Today – Christened a small nigger 'Skittles', he is a most ugly specimen of humanity so I shall know him again. Tucker gave me his Mosquito net – Thank God I shall not have the trouble of making one now. Gave him a Letter of introduction to Hart, wrote to D, also Home. Am going to take up three bottles of PB for the Giant[92] in my swag. Could do a Comfortable loaf here for a few days.

Blank.

FRIDAY, MAY 21ST, 1875 ~ Turned out about 8.30, Hot Coppers[93]. Got a little above burning heat last night. Snored like an Alligator all night, Mr. Blood obliged to take Laudanum to go to sleep. Pretty state of things, this. Expect to get away from here before dinner. Horses, with one exception, are all in the Yard. 5 PM. After keeping Horses in nearly all day, we were obliged to turn them out again as men have not yet found the missing Horse. The Peake people will again have the pleasure of being kept awake by my night performances.

Curled up about 11.30.

SATURDAY, MAY 22ND ~ Got up about 7.50, one of my fingers rather sore from the effects of a bite given as a remedy against Snoring. Cannot appreciate this kind of kindness. 2 PM, after drinking Mr. and Mrs. Blood's health, we started – our party consists of four riding horses and two pack. Saw a lot of niggers at the Peake Creek about 2 miles N of the station and amongst the Mob, I noticed a little half-Caste Girl[94] who was very fair indeed, in fact if she were Cleaned and dressed properly it would be very difficult to distinguish her from a dark-complexioned Child of the same age. Saw half a dozen native women in the Neale's Creek[95] – they had half a dozen Lizards (native name – Cadney) on the Coals, roasting for their evening meal. They possessed one old Blanket between them and were all as nature Clothed them! Shocking! Travelled until 8.30 and Camped at a small waterhole on the Ockington Flat[96] in which there were a great number of fresh water bream. This water is not permanent and is now nearly dry. The fish are supposed to breed after every rain, from the spawn left in the hole. Made some Buggers[97] on the Coal for Tea, also a Johnnie Cake[98] for breakfast tomorrow.

~

92 the Giant – The Giant of the Interior was Ebenezer Flint, who received a severe spear wound in the thigh during the attack on Barrow Creek O.T. Station on 23 February, 1874 when the station master John Stapleton and lineman John Frank were killed by Aboriginal people.

93 Hot Coppers – parched throat to be expected after a drinking bout.

94 little half-Caste Girl – It might just be be possible that she was Mary Smith, mother of Topsy Smith and grandmother of Walter Smith (Dick Kimber).

95 Neale's Creek – named after John Bentham Neales, parliamentarian.

96 Ockington Flat – Ockenden Spring and Creek, named after William Marshall Ockenden who worked on the Peake pastoral run and eventually joined the police force.

97 Buggers – politely known as 'beggars'. A thinnish cake speckled with currants and baked hastily on the glowing embers.

98 Johnnie Cake – similar to damper but closer in size to a scone, basically flour and water. It is cooked in the ashes or in a pan (P. Jones).

Carted myself into the Blankets at 11.10. Loaded my Shooting *Iron*![99]

SUNDAY, MAY 23RD, 1875 ~ Turned out 7 AM. Managed to catch a fish. Skinner Cooked it. Our Johnnie Cake turned out a sad failure – being what is generally called a Bishop's Sod. Made a start about 8.15. Met waggon at Hann's Creek[100] where we spelled a Couple of hours and had dinner. Now travelling through Stuart's Stoney Desert[101] – like this Country for travelling much better than that South of the Peake – the Scenery is much prettier and not so monotonous – travelled 23 Miles and Camped on the Cecelia Creek.

Turned in about 7.15.

MONDAY, MAY 24TH, 1875 ~ Her Majesty's Birthday. Made a start about 8.30. Had to Go about 2 miles after the Horses – Travelled thro' some nice Country. Caught a Lizard and cut his tail and hind legs off. Bob and I are going to cook him tonight, we are looking forward to a treat! Arrived at the Angle Pole[102], 15 miles from last night's Camp, about 12.30. Had some dinner, put in at the Shackle[103] and spoke to Peake. A Couple of Niggers, one nicely painted, Came from the Scrub and had a yabber with us. Gave them some bacca – they were both perfectly naked, one Man had a wreath around his head made out of the tail of a Wild dog. They had been out hunting and had a wooden trough nearly full of Lizards, roots and a very large and peculiar species of frogs. One of them told me I was a white Blackfellow when I told him I intended Cooking a Cadney for tea! Made a fresh start about 2.15, travelled through some very nice looking Country and Camped on the Storm Creek – a distance of 33 miles from last night's Camp. Found a nest of Shell parrots[104] in a tree close to the Camp & as I had no means of carting them, let the poor little Devils rip. Cooked the Lizard's tail and, as we are rather badly-off for meat, it Came in handy.

Coiled 9[105].

TUESDAY, MAY 25TH, 1875 ~ Turned out 6.15, Cold as Charity. Good fire kept up all night. Made a start about 7.45. Crossed the Macumba Creek[106] in which there are several fine large waterholes and stopped at the Stevenson[107] for

~

99 Gillen was aware that for some considerable time, Peake had been known as the edge of the frontier, so it was worth taking some extra precautions. At this time the Peake station was known as the best source for recruiting native police, trackers, etc. for outback Australia. This is possibly because the Aboriginal people there had retained their bush skills and tracking abilities and also had an appreciation of European life coupled with a distrust of the 'wild' bush Aborigines (P. Jones).

100 Hann's Creek – refers to the explorer William Hann.

101 Stuart's Stoney Desert – named informally after the explorer Stuart. The name was never officially recognised (P Jones).

102 Angle Pole – a placename. It is very close to Oodnadatta and denotes a sharp turn that the telegraph line takes at the spot which local people designated Carulinia.

103 put in at the Shackle – to put in the instrument to make a connection to the O.T. Line so that a message could be sent.

104 Shell parrots – budgerigars (*Melopsittacus undulatus*).

105 Coiled 9 – went to bed at 9.

106 Macumba Creek – Mucca-umba, 'fire come on', discovered by Stephen Jarvis in 1862. In fact, at this part of the creek it is known as the Alberga Creek. It is called the Macumba downstream of the Stevenson junction.

107 Stevenson – was discovered by Stuart in 1860 and named after Charles E. Stevenson, a member of the firm of Hunter and Stevenson, merchants of Grenfell Street, Adelaide. Stevenson married the elder sister of Andrew Tennant, pastoralist and legislator. Local Aboriginal people knew the river as Ooljeraginia.

Dinner. Saddled up and made a fresh start at 1.30. Travelled through some very stony Country and Camped at Block Camp – where there is a good-sized waterhole. Wish I was in Adelaide to see the Cup[108] run for today. I fancy "Echo" will be first horse. We made a regular old-Man fire[109] and Cooked a Couple of Dampers in the Ashes. They turned out first-Class.

Wint [sic] 2 bed 9. Big fire burning to warm our toes.

WEDNESDAY, MAY 26TH, 1875 ~ Tumbled out 6 AM. Got in our Mokes[110], had Scram and started at 20 minutes to 8. Travelled through sand and stony Country. Saw some Niggers' tracks in the Sand. Halted at a waterhole Called "The Three Forges", on account of it being an old Shoeing Camp. Made a stay of about an hour and a half, then saddled up and started again. Passed a Group of waterholes called "The Box Swamp"[111] Saw a very pretty wild pigeon[112], the plumage excels anything I have yet seen in this part of the Country. We are getting short of Meat and jam – expect to have to live on dry Damper for a day or so. This will not tend to increase my weight. 5.15. Arrived at Southers Creek where we Camped for the Night. Very little water here and what there is, is Brackish.

Fell into the blankets 8.30.

THURSDAY, MAY 27TH, 1875 ~ Jumped out of Blankets 6 AM. Cold as Blazes. Had breakfast about 7 and started at 7.45. Travelling through stony and very hilly Country. Scenery in some places, very good. Getting tired of the saddle and shall not growl much when I reach my destination, it feels like hard work travelling 30 Miles a day. Saw some very small birds in a Red Mulga Creek[113], believe they are Humming Birds. Spelled at the Opossum Waterhole for a Couple of hours and had dinner. Finished the last of our Salt Horse and Jam. We go on Prison Tack until we arrive at Charlotte Waters[114]. Made a fresh start about 2 PM. Travelled through Sandy Country, saw a very large Lagoon where there is a fine sheet of water. Bird's nests are very plentiful in the Sandhills. I Counted 14 nests in a small Mulga tree. Camped on the Hughes Creek[115] where Mr. Knucky[116] camped with his party for some time. There is a Cattle and Sheep yard here, also three or four

~

108 the Cup – The Adelaide Cup (Echo didn't run). The Adelaide Cup was run over a distance of 2 miles and was won by Lurline, a five-year-old bay mare owned by J. Watts. The purse was 250 sovereigns and a piece of plate valued at 100 sovereigns was presented by Hon. T. Elder M.L.C.

109 old-Man fire – a larger than usual fire.

110 Mokes – conventional slang for 'horses'.

111 The Box Swamp – named after the box gums (coolibah – *Eucalyptus microtheca*) of the locality.

112 wild pigeon – probably spinifex pigeon (*Petrophasic plumifera*).

113 Red Mulga Creek – named for the colour of the bark, which curls. Aranda name for Red Mulga tree is 'minnaritji'. (*Acacia cyperophylla*).

114 Charlotte Waters – named for Lady Charlotte Mary Bacon, daughter of the Earl of Oxford and a friend of Lord Byron. Byron dedicated his 'Childe Harold's Pilgrimage' to her. Alexander Tolmer inscribed his two volumes of reminiscences to her. He relates a story that Lady Bacon used to tell against herself. She was visiting Melbourne and, in directing a porter what to do with her luggage labelled 'Lady Charlotte Bacon', said 'You won't forget the name will you?' The porter answered naively, 'No mum, it's not likely, because my name's Hog'.

115 Hughes Creek – possibly named after a teamster who discovered it at about the time of the O.T. construction.

116 Mr. Knucky – R.R. Knuckey, a member of North–South Transcontinental Telegraph construction party of 1870–72. In 1877 he also completed the South Australian portion of the telegraph line to Western Australia.

ANGLE POLE, MOUNT TODMORDEN, 1908

Mortlock Library: SSL:M:B47898

CHARLOTTE WATERS

This sketch is the 'plan' Gillen refers to on page 68.

Wurleys[117] – Water permanent – distance travelled, 31 Miles. Made some Beggars on the Coals for tea – they tasted rather dry. Made an old Man fire so as to have plenty Ashes to Cook a damper in the morning. Expect to reach Charlotte Waters tomorrow night.

Koiled [sic] up 9 pm.

FRIDAY, MAY 28TH, 1875 ~ Turned out 6 AM. Awfully Cold, had some trouble in finding Horses. Cooked some Johnnie Cakes and made a start about 8, travelled through some beastly stony Country. Crossed the Abminga Creek[118] in two places and Camped on the North side for Dinner which we did not particularly enjoy! Saw several Niggers in the scrub including a juvenile half Caste. Two of the Men came over to have a look at us and got some tobacco for their Curiosity. Saw half a dozen old Wigwams on the South Bank of the Abminga, they had evidently not been inhabited for some time. Saddled up and started again at 2 PM. Country stony – Arrived at Charlotte Waters Station about 5.30 PM. My stern blistered and am jolly glad to get out of the pigskin for a day or two. Mr. Giles the Station Master is away on the Line[119], am sorry for this, as I should have liked to have seen him. The office here is really a Credit to the worthy S.M.[120] Everything is in pin

~

117 Wurleys – according to G. Taplin in *The Native Tribes of South Australia*, 1879, the word 'wurley' means a native hut in the language of the Adelaide tribe.

118 Abminga Creek – abminga means 'a snake track'. The course of the creek was regarded by local Aboriginal people as the track of a mythical snake.

119 away on the Line – travelling along the O.T. Line in the course of his job.

120 S.M. – station master.

Cushion order. The Telegraph Department may well be proud of such an excellent Officer. The Police Trooper here informs me that while he was absent a few days ago, the Natives mustered in large numbers, all painted up and fully armed with Spears and Boomerangs as if meditating an attack on the Station, directly they saw him returning, they dispersed. The Station is built on a large bare plain, there is not even a bush to be seen within at least half a mile. The house is, in appearance, very much like a Gaol. The only entrance is at the back.

See plan below. [See page 66.]

SATURDAY, MAY 29TH, 1875 ~ Was aroused by the magic word 'Breakfast' at 8 AM. After scram Bob and I went for a stroll and bargained with a Couple of Gins to wash our Clothes – which they did in a very unsatisfactory manner. My invalid Stern progressing favorably. The Natives here call the Trooper "The Knifey whitefellow". Christened three very small Nigger Boys respectively – "Monday", "Friday" and "Bawley". The worthy parents seemed highly pleased. Cleaned my Revolver up a bit and had a trial shot or two. Mended my Moleskin bricks[121]. Start for Alice Springs as early as possible tomorrow morning. The Natives here, when in Mourning, mix pipeclay with their hair. There is one old Girl at the Station who has recently lost some relative, she is ugly at her best but with the pipeclayed hair she is positively hideous.

SUNDAY, MAY 30TH, 1875 ~ Got up about 7. Native Boy "Billy" started out after the Horses at daylight. Horses brought in about 12, saddled up, had Dinner and made a start at 12.50. Truly, I am the most unfortunate poor Devil under the Sun. If there is a Vicious Horse to be got, I am bound to drop in for it. The one I am now riding, I got at Charlotte Waters. Her particular weakness is Kicking other Horses. She Kicked at Bob's Charger this PM and landed him one on the Big Toe. Trooper McBeth accompanied us for 8 or 9 miles – Followed the Line until dark. Country very scrubby. Saw the Smoke of a Nigger's fire in the distance. Bob's Charger and one of the Pack Horses got bogged in the "Goyder Creek"[122]. Bob managed to get his Nag out OK but we had some trouble in releasing The Pack Horse. Camped on the left Bank of the above-named Creek. Distance travelled 35 miles. Arrived at Camp 8 PM. Hungry as an Alligator.

MONDAY, MAY 31ST, 1875 ~ Turned out 6.30, very Chilly. Breakfasted & made a start at 8.10. When we arrived at the Finke[123], Bob discovered his revolver missing. Skinner and he immediately started back to last night's Camp,

~

121 Moleskin bricks – moleskin breeks (trousers).

122 Goyder Creek – George Woodroofe Goyder CMG, named as one of South Australia's twelve greatest men, was born in 1824 in Liverpool and educated in Glasgow. During the drought of 1865 he made his name imperishable by delineating Goyder's Line of Rainfall, which still holds good as defining the safe demarcation for agricultural operation. He died on 2 November, 1898.

123 Finke Creek – perpetuates the memory of William Finke. He prospered as a pastoralist and was associated with John and James Chambers in promoting the great exploration work of John McDouall Stuart. The Aboriginal name for Finke River is Lirambenda: lira – creek and mbenda – permanent water or spring. It was first recorded, though, as Larapinta, and this spelling prevails (e.g. Larapinta Drive, Alice Springs).

a distance of 12 miles. Hanley[124] and I took pack Horses on to the Green Waterhole, Finke Creek and camped. Country scrubby & sandy. Scenery beautiful. The Finke is the largest Creek I have seen since leaving Adelaide. Its banks are well-timbered, principally with red Gum. 2 PM, Bob and Joe returned having found the missing Mucketa[125] about five miles back. Bob not atall well. Started again at 2.30, followed up the Creek for 2 or 3 miles. Scenery beautiful. Arrived at the Crossing of the Finke Creek at dusk. Distance travelled 35 miles.

TUESDAY, JUNE 1ST, 1875 ~ Turned out 6 AM. Got Horses in and made a start about 8. Tom Hanley found a Bottle of Pale Brandy, Hennessey's best, in the bed of the Creek. It had evidently been dropped by some travellers. Travelled thro' some nice Country and watered our Horses at the Finke;, a very fine Creek. 11.15 AM, camped for dinner and etc. Opened the Bottle and found the Liquor A1. After stowing away some Grilled Chops, started again at 1.15. Country very sandy. Arrived at Horseshoe Bend (on the Finke) 5 pm, where we met Mr. Giles of Charlotte Waters. Finished the bottle of PB before tea. When I opened my Swag, found one Bottle of Flint's Brandy missing. Of course this acccounted for us finding one this AM. Felt much disgusted. Bob did up my Swag this morning in a most Careless manner, or this loss would not have occurred. My surprise on finding there was a bottle missing created some merriment. Saw some of Stuart's pigeons[126], they are very pretty birds, having bronze wings and a very long topknot sticking straight up on the head. Distance travelled about 28 miles.

WEDNESDAY, JUNE 2ND, 1875 ~ Turned out 6.30 AM. Got two fresh Horses from Mr. Giles and started at 8.45. Travelled the Old Depot Sandhills[127], which are very heavy indeed. Followed the Line, leaving the Main track to the left, for 8 or 10 miles. Country very rough for travelling through but scenery beautiful. Crossed the Hugh[128] in two or three places and arrived at Alice Creek[129], 2.15 PM where we met Mr. P. Egerton Warburton and party, also Mr. Giles' Line repairing party. Distance travelled about 25 miles. Spoke to AG[130] about 4 PM from the Alice Creek shackle.

THURSDAY, JUNE 3RD, 1875 ~ Turned out about 5.30. Cold enough to freeze the Nose off a brass Monkey. The water in our waterbags frozen quite hard. A panikin [sic] of water that I left near my Shakedown before retiring last night was frozen through. It is much Colder in this part of the Country

~

124 Hanley – Tom Hanley was with the party which surveyed the route in 1870. He also travelled with Ernest Giles from Lake Eyre, westerly through the Great Victorian Desert.
125 Mucketa – Aboriginal English for 'gun'.
126 Stuart's pigeons – Spinifex pigeons (*Petrophasia plumifera*).
127 Old Depot Sandhills – take their name from an O.T. Line Depot established close to the Finke River–Hugh River junction during the course of construction of the O.T. Line.
128 the Hugh – creek named after Hugh Chambers.
129 Alice Creek – possibly named by John Ross, who explored ahead of the O.T. Line crews in 1870–71.
130 AG – Telegraph code for Alice Springs.

than it is in Adelaide. Made a start about 7.45. Travelling through sandy, scrubby and hilly Country until about 12.15, when we spelled for dinner at The Francis Creek. Whilst we were having dinner, about a dozen or fifteen Natives came into our Camp and, after dropping their spears, Boomerangs etc., commenced to Yabber. One of the men could speak a few words of English. They were all as Nature clothed them, one old Buffer, who appeared to be a Big Gun, was smeared from head to foot with yellow ochre. I named a Couple of the Piccaninnies "Sunday" and "Sally". They gave us to understand that they were members of the "Coomarrie"[131] Tribe. Some of the youngsters had a piece of stick through the Nose. Cannot imagine what this is for. Started again at 1.20. Passed the Grave of Mr. Kraegen, the Operator who died through want of water in 1871. The Grave is neatly fenced in and there is a Headstone of Granite erected, which bears the following inscription:-

> "To the Memory of C.W.J. Kraegen, Who died from Exhaustion, through want of water, on or about December 17th, '71."

Travelled through some first rate Country, Grassy plains with low ranges of Hills on both sides of the track. Camped at a Claypan about 3 miles South of the Deep Crossing. Distance travelled about 45 miles. We are camped about 100 yards to the left of the track. Water not permanent. Forgot to mention that Bob and I had a narrow escape of being Bushed. Skinner and our Guide, who were ahead some distance, went off the track, and we, missing their tracks, got quite out of our reckoning.

FRIDAY, JUNE 4TH, 1875 ~ Turned out about 6. Awfully cold. Started about 8 AM. Crossed the Kraegen Creek (large waterhole about half a mile up the Creek from the Crossing – water generally to be depended upon). Travelling though scrubby Country, spelled on the Hugh for Dinner. After taking in a fair Cargo of Damper and Mutton, saddled up and made a fresh start at 1.30. Country very scrubby but pleasant to travel through. Passed through the James Ranges[132] which are very steep and Rocky, they extend for some considerable distance. Spinifex and Desert Oak plentiful. Crossed the Doctor's Creek[133] before coming to the Ranges. There is a waterhole under some large rocks, about 200 yards from the Crossing. Had a look at the Grave of a Native who was shot about 2 years since by a man named Webb. The Nigger had been stealing some of Webb's provisions and also attempted to spear him. I noticed the tracks of two blacks near the Grave, they had evidently been doing it up. Camped on the Hugh. Some Natives visited us in the evening. None of them could speak English – one old Bird however, styled himself 'Major Warburton' and was, he informed us, the happy Husband of two gushing young Lubras who accompanied him to our Camp.

~

131 Coomarrie – undoubtedly Gillen's rendering of one of the four Lower Aranda class or section names – Kumarre (P. Jones).

132 James Ranges – named after James Chambers. John and James Chambers were patrons of John McDouall Stuart, the explorer.

133 Doctor's Creek – named for Doctor Freidrich Emil Renner who was with O.T. Line crews in the early 1870s. Also Renner's Springs.

They had a picanninie[134] [sic] each. This speaks well for the Major. Made my first Damper.

SATURDAY, JUNE 5TH, 1875 ~ Roused out at daylight. A mob of nigs visited us at 6.30, all Carrying firesticks. Made a start about 8. We were delayed through Horses having rambled during the night. Had a look at McClures Springs. These springs are formed in the bed of the Hugh Creek and were named after Bob's Dad by Mr. Stuart, the Explorer. Was shown a large tree in the Creek on which Stuart had cut his initials. Travelling through the James and Waterhouse Ranges[135] until 1 o'clock when we arrived at Gilbert's Station[136], 42 miles South of the Alice. Spoke to Alice Springs[137] from the Shackle. After having a festive old feed, started for "Millners Camp"[138] on the Hugh, where we camped for the night. My Damper very great success.

SUNDAY, JUNE 6TH, 1875 ~ Got up before the lark this morning. I started at 8.20, rest of party detained through two of the Horses having gone on the back track. Harris and Conlon met us at Fenn's Gap where we spelled for dinner. Saddled up and started again at 2. The Giant of the Interior met us at Temple Bar with a four-in-hand waggonette and a musician in the shape of a small Buck Nigger who played the Cornet. I took a seat in the trap. Our festive whip got pitched out and had a narrow escape of being run over. Had his wind knocked out. Arrived at Alice Springs 5 PM. Station very nicely situated. It is right in the heart of the McDonnell Ranges[139]. Blank!

To The Reader.

This Diary was commenced shortly after leaving Adelaide with a view of giving my Metropolitan friends a rough sketch of my first Campaign in the Bush and a slight description of the General Character and principal features of the Country we travelled through. Our party with two or three exceptions were comparatively new to Bush Life and after the first few days travelling had shaken things pretty well into working order, the beautiful weather, bright Cloudless days and starlight nights (which however after the first two or three weeks were quite cool enough to be pleasant), perhaps induced us to take rather a rose coloured view of what, under different Circumstances, might have produced a song, which your humble Servant – the unworthy mouthpiece of the Party – would have sung in a totally different Key. As however, Jove, who, being the first

~

134 picanninie – Colloquial term for Aboriginal baby.

135 Waterhouse Ranges – F.J. Waterhouse was the naturalist on Stuart's last (successful) expedition. He was curator of the Adelaide Museum and the discoverer of the famous parakeet, Princess Alexandria Parrot (*Polytelis alexandrae*).

136 Gilbert's Station – Owen Springs cattle station owned by William Gilbert, son of Joseph who arrived in South Australia 21 March 1839 and established a property at Pewsey Vale.

137 Alice Springs – named after Lady Todd, wife of Sir Charles Todd.

138 Millner's Camp – named for Ralph Milner, the first man to take sheep from southern Australia (actually Killalpaninna Mission on the Cooper) to the north coast. This epic journey is described in *The Territory*, by Ernestine Hill, and took place during 1870, just before the Overland Telegraph party went through on the same route (P. Jones).

139 McDonnell Ranges – after Sir Richard Graves MacDonnell, Governor of South Australia 1855–62, who was born in Dublin, the son of Rev. Dr MacDonnell, Provost of Trinity College, Dublin. In 1847 he married Blanche, daughter of Francis Skurray. He was given the honorary degree of L.L.D. by Trinity College in 1844.

Lightning Squirter, we assume to be the protecting genius of latter-day Telegraph Officials, was kind enough to use his influence in our favour, we had, on the whole, a pleasant journey. I think that, although the motives which influenced us individually in thus pressing outward through the boundaries of Civilization and Settlement would at the first glance be ascribed to different sources in each Individual case, yet I think a deeper scrutiny would soon convince you that as usual they spring from that Great mainspring which keeps in motion, we may say, the whole machinery by which Mother Earth, or rather Mother Earth's Sons wag along, the circulating Medium by which Commerce is maintained, nations brought into amicable competition and friendly intercourse and for which Mankind is indebted for civilization, tea meetings, teetotalism, Morley punshionism[140] and other blessings too numerous to mention, had excersised [sic] its influence on three poor Devils of Telegraph operators, Money, Money, Monish one wanting a start in the world, one wanting a wife, the other hardly knowing what he wants himself, but Money, Money, Money, the cry of all. And seriously speaking, the Bush without doubt affords the best opportunity for the saving Man, who to acquire the slippery needful is willing to forgo the pleasures of Town Life, Feminine Society, et hoc genus omne, and buckle down to work. The inconveniences of Bush Life, which are very trying at first to the uninitiated, are considered as comparatively trifling after association with them; & a few years Steady Industry will place the Saving Man in a fair position to make a fair Start on his own account in almost any

PETER EGERTON WARBURTON c.1874

Mortlock Library: SSL:M:B7938

TELEGRAPH STATION ALICE SPRINGS

SKETCH BY W. POUNSETT, 1876

Mortlock Library: SSL:M:B25062

FOUNDATION STONE AT FIRST POST OFFICE – ALICE SPRINGS

Courtesy Post Office Museum

business he prefers. I would however impress upon whoever by perusing these Lines should be induced to try their fortune in the South Australian Interior – whether in the OT or otherwise – to think over the few following suggestions before jumping out of the Frying pan into the fire, as he will find by experience, that this – like all other mundane avocations – has its drawbacks, and to use a familiar phrase, is not all "Beer and Skittles".

1st, Start young. The years which you waste in Town on a small salary barely sufficient to support you, may be spent more profitably in every way, and money saved, in the Bush.

2nd, Don't come unless you make up your mind to save Money, for you can fool it away easily enough even in the Bush, so that your volantary [sic] Exile in such a Case would be fruitless.

3rd, Bring a sound Constitution, a Civil Tongue, cleanly habits and a willingness to learn & rough it a bit – or don't come atall.

4th, Make up your mind to learn the outside as well as perform the inside work on a Station, or you will be a most useless, helpless Animal.

In Conclusion, I may state that these few Lines are not written with any other Idea than that Contained in the first page of this preface and if any of my admiring friends look over this with an Eye to publish, or propose making the Gifted

~

140 Morley punshionism – a reference to Methodism. The term was popularised in the satirical Adelaide journal, *Pasquin*, during the later 1860s (P. Jones).

Author a presentation of a silver teapot or any other small but valuable token of esteem, they will find the said G.A. quite willing to receive the same and give the aforesaid appreciative individuals an oportunity of showing their sentiments in a graceful manner. Should I be allowed a Choice, I might mention that a Statue in Victoria Square would fully meet my wishes in the matter.

Trusting that the above may be not only the means of passing away an Idle hour but that my experiences may be of service to any among you who may wish to follow in my footsteps or strike out a new Line for themselves.

I wish you all, readers & friends, whether in S.A. or Elsewhere, Good Bye & Good Luck.

Yrs,

The Author

Word List A

Corremi	Come on
Auru	Yes
Badnie	No
Minella	What
Mucketa	Revolver [Aboriginal pronunciation of Musket]
Unkitcha	Moon
Arlinga	The Sun
An-tur-bura	The Stars
Oora	Wood (Fire)
Quir-la-agga	Young woman
Wee-ya	Boy
Il-charda	A spear
Ur-tee-ta	Teeth
Eel-pucka-ta	Ear

~

Gillen headed this list, pencilled in the first two pages of his journal, with the title, 'Nigger Vocabulary'. It appears to consist mainly of Arabana, and possibly Wangkangurru, words, and would represent the earliest record of those languages (P. Jones and L. Hercus).

Urrr-ipa-tchauia	Three
Thram-a-binna	Four
Um-brickack-nictia	Very fat white man
Al-poo-tcha	Shell parrot
Woon-da	Fish
Ong-er-la	A Crow
Urr-leah	Emu
Ug-gurrah	Kangaroo
Art-nimma	crying
Ur-ning-ya	Whiskers
Ack-eera	Hair
Waroo	An old man
Oourla oula	An old woman
Nutla	Young man, blackfellow
Parracoola Milleru	Two, or a pair
Neoyu	One
Kulparrie	Three
Walpa	All about
Murrearie	Teal duck
Mudlyappa	Wild dog
Morra	A hand
Tidna	Foot
Meena	Eye
Moodla	Nose
Curteyab	Head
Mucca	Fire
Wirra	A tree

Niccee	Here
Larra	A creek
Burrabburra	Very big
Wabma	Snake
Cadney	Jew Lizard
Cobrie	Iguana
Cootha	water
Mundowie	A track
Whityarra	Which way

Names of Natives, N of Peake

Male	*Female*
Adnella	Artey bornicka
Noor-licka	Oodningi
Oort-noom-orca	Ipadeequa
	(E-pad-ee-qua)
Alta-balta	Aranellica
At-yadda	Illabrica
Lu-ar-a-nu	Meningie
E-yib-a-da	Ipeteybunckceta
Ar-lu-kill-yicca	Mil-chee-cur-dah
Obejie	Cul-yan-dan-eca
Untam-in-narra	Ar-rip-ica
Ock-at-ad-ricka	Ab-ma-ooca
Carra-min-dica	Ood-ning-ya
Oob-num-bica	Ah-la-whit-yarra
An-thia-lia	Mun-de-larrie
Oort-nan-jee-ca	
Che-Cellia	

Word List B

Al-lelia	Grass
Apra	Gum tree
Al-linga	A long distance
Anima	Sit down
Al-lick-ena	Where
Ar-linga	The sun
An-tur-bura	The stars
Al-poo-tcha	Shell parrot
Art-nimma	Crying
Ack-eera	Hair
App-ertie	Stone
Arn-bricka	Centepede [sic]
At-nit-therta	Scorpion
At-thong-in-thong-ya	Do you want it?
An-ke-de-lud-ne-ma	Thirsty
Ack-rill-ima	Lightning

~

Gillen titled this list, written in ink at the back of his journal, 'Vocabulary of Native Language'. It follows the list of Aboriginal names collected north of Peake station and contains Lower Aranda words, several of which correspond to those later collected by Gillen at Charlotte Waters Telegraph Station and published in Curr (1886–87). This is the earliest known record of Lower Aranda (P. Jones).

Anga-im-panya	It is raining
A-kurra	Flesh of any kind
Ack-oolia	Hair
Ar-tee-ta	Teeth
Ar roc-er-ta	Mouth
Algana	Eye
Ar-tip-pa	The back
Ad-nur-te-la	The seat
Ara-pull-a	The lips
Ara-nilla	Sit down
Ang-wah-kurting	Night
At-tike-a	Dawn of day
Ang-war-illa	Today
Ang-war-illa-He-at-la	Tonight
Al-cher-ka	Tomorrow
Ar-tock-ar-ta	The heart
An-ter-pre-ma	To laugh
At-thong-e-wah	I want it
Al-mer ta	Very nice
Atha-in-al-pal-pa	I'll bring it
Al-lan-jee-ler-ta	I think so
Chil-ka	Meat
Coon-ga-ra	Sister
Coo-ler-la	Yes
Cam-minna	Uncle
Cul-lorr	Going for
E-lip-pa	A noise

Eng-won-ter-pe-la	The day after tomorrow
Err-a-qua	You hold it
E-tra-tha-pitch-cha	Be quick
Heed-na-nitch-a	To lose
Inga	A footprint
Il-cher-da	A spear
Indama or Onquo	Sleeping
Onqua	Sleeping
Il-jer-ka	Tomorrow morning
Ing-nim-tim	Bleeding
Ing-nur-na	The leg
In-ka	The foot
It-ha	The neck
Inta-lock-a-low	Lie down
Ir-ock-wah	To be silent
In-te-jah	Unwell
It-hoor-ra	Hard or strong
Ip-al-an-hanta	Every day
Ib-min-itcha	Mother
In-gwurr-na	Bone
Il-pock-ar-ta	The ear
It-in-ja	The arms
Intha	The thigh
Ip-ling-urra	Very soon
Kill-a	Allright
Mon-jick-Ill-lil-la	Be careful, don't fall

Matina	Mother
Moona	Food
Murtha	A great number
Mum-ma	A woman's breasts
Man-ke	A lie
Myrka-Il-cher-ka	Yesterday
Nobe-ly	Like it
Nitch-inda	Stand up
Nee-im-la-ma	Heat
Nil-lum	Giddy
Oon-neeca	My or mine
Ool-ker ma	Eating
Ock-nee-ya	Father
Ock-kil-yocki	Brother
Og-nee-ler-la	Grandfather
Ock-op-er-la	The Head
Or-uck-ur-ick-na	The Skull
Ock-um-erra	Get up
Oo-larra	The Track
Oonga-In-al-pal-pa	You bring it to me
Ong-wurd-er-pee-la	Night before last
Ool-qul-la	Thunder
Ong-i	You
Ock-oc-koo-lema	Sleepy
Pulla	The skin
Thrama	Two
Thram-ur-pin	Three

Urd-nimma	To cry or scream
Ul-tin-la	Perspiring
Um-bra	The knee
Ul-ta-nilla	All day
Un-door-ra	Fat
Ur-a-wa	Go away
Un-eng-ge-lid-nema	Hungry
Un-din-ye-la	Rain
Un Che-ma	Drinking
Ur-nammi	Grass
Wur-ne-ma	Wind
Won-am-le-lya	I don't want it
Wher-ti-abba	A road
Yenga	I
Yunda	One
Thongi	Get out of the way
Ar-incha-Lawooma	Very cold

Appendix

from *Gillen's Diary: The Camp Jottings of F.J. Gillen*

MAY 17TH, 1901 ~ Camp No. 22. Ter. Min. 27.
A delightfully bracing morning, one feels very much alive on such a morning. Had breakfast and reached Station at 8. Writing and doing odd jobs all day. Spencer began his *Age* articles and has ground away at them all day. Had party's photo taken but it is not good of Spencer or the boys so we intend trying another tomorrow. Chance busy making cases to pack native implements of which we have quite a goodly store. Decided not to leave here until after arrival of mail on 21st.; we have plenty of work on hand to keep us engaged until then. It is a comfort to me to know that I shall get another mail without having to wait weeks for it. Tom Hanley who is one of my oldest friends in the Interior and under whose wing I made my first entrance into Bush life arrived from the North today: time is beginning to tell upon him – he is grey and gnarled looking; a trifle more cynical but still the same splendid type of hardy bushman. We are delighted to meet again and some pleasant hours are spent in reminiscing. I find it hard to realise that it is 25 years since he first introduced me to camp life at a spot about 10 miles north of the present Beltana township

which then consisted only of a Telegraph Station. What changes have been effected since then; it is marvellous. At that time the Northern railway system terminated at the Burra from whence we travelled by a badly-horsed and rickety coach to Blinman which was then quite a prosperous bush township. From the Blinman we travelled to Beltana by hired trap which was driven by an old Blinman identity rejoicing in the name of Jimmy Duck who still flourishes in the Leigh Creek locality. Horses had been sent to meet us from Strangways Springs and one, a young bay colt, was allotted to me. The man who broke him in brought the horses down and assured me that my mount was as quiet as a lamb, spirited and playful as a respectable young horse should be "but no vice Mister you can take it from me". I saddled him up and at once experienced some of his playfulness in the shape of a sharp nip which deprived me of portion of my shirt. I began to funk and mildly suggested that his eye looked wicked whereupon my friend the breaker mumbling something about limejuicers and with a look of scorn took hold of the reins, gripped the beast's ear with one hand and saying "Whoa my pretty!" threw himself lightly into the saddle; in an instant the playful viceless animal had assumed the position depicted above and for 10 solid, and to me awful, minutes he made frantic efforts to turn himself inside out, then, exhausted with his efforts, he stopped and the Breaker patting his neck and saying "good little hoss" got off and led the brute up to me remarking "what more do you want Mister, aint he a bloomin lamb, no vice, you see he didn't squeal once". I said "Thanks I'll ride in the wagon" and

I did for several days until some of the "playfulness" had been knocked out of him. At last I mustered up courage to mount him one afternoon, he had been ridden all morning. I remained in the saddle just three minutes and for the rest of the day travelled in the Ambulance. Returned to camp at 9 p.m. Bar. An. S.T.

Bibliography for Footnotes

Ackerman, R., *J.F. Frazer – His life and Work* (Cambridge University Press), 1990.

Auhl, I., *Burra – The Story of the Monster Mine* (Investigator Press, Adelaide), 1986.

Australian Dictionary of Biography (Melbourne University Press), 1968.

Baker, S., *The Australian Language* (Currawong Press, Sydney), 1966.

Blackwell, D. & Lockwood, D., *Alice on the Line* (Rigby, Adelaide), 1965.

Cawte, J. et al, *The Meaning of Subincision of the Urethra to Aboriginal Australians* (British Journal of Medical Psychology) (1966), p 39, p 245.

Cockburn, R., *What's in a Name?* (Ferguson Publications, Adelaide), 1984.

Curr, E.M. (ed.), *The Australian Race,* (John Ferres, Melbourne), Gillen, F.J. 1886–87. Charlotte Waters Telegraph Station (Vocabulary) in, vol. 1, pp. 418–19.

Dickens, C., *"The Pickwick Papers" – Guide to English Literature* (Prentice Hall), 1990.

Freud, S., *Totem and Taboo*, (Routledge and Kegan Paul, London), 1950, p 114.

Gillen, F.J., *Gillen's Diary: The Camp Jottings of F.J. Gillen*, (South Australian Libraries Board), 1968.

Gillen, F.J. & Spencer, W.B., *The Native Tribes of Central Australia* (Macmillan, London), 1899.

Hill, E., *The Territory* (Ure Smith, Sydney), 1970.

Kempe, H., *Participation* (Hawthorn Press, Melbourne), 1973.

Loyau, G., *Notable South Australians* (Carey, Paget and Co., Adelaide), 1985.

Manning, G.H., *The Romance of Place Names of South Australia* (Gillingham Printers, Adelaide), 1989.

Marret, R.R. & Penniman, T.K. (eds), *Spencer's Scientific Correspondence with Sir J.G. Frazer and Others* (Clarendon Press, Oxford), 1932.

Mincham, H., *The Story of the Flinders Ranges* (Rigby, Adelaide), 1964.

1000 Famous Australians (Rigby, Adelaide), 1978.

Pasquin

Partridge, E., *The Penguin Dictionary of Historical Slang* (Penguin, London), 1972.

Petrick, J., *The History of Alice Springs Through Street Names* (Graphic Services, Northfield, South Australia), 1989.

The Register

Richardson, N.A., *Pioneers of the North West of South Australia* (Libraries Board of South Australia), 1969.

Scherer, P.A., *A Venture of Faith – An Epic in Australian Missionary History* (Board of the Finke River Mission of the United Evangelical Lutheran Church in Australia, Tanunda, South Australia), 1964 2nd impression.

Stapleton, A., *Willshire of Alice Springs* (Hesperian Press, Western Australia), 1992.

Stuart, J.McD., *The Journals of John McDouall Stuart* (Saunders, Otley & Co, London), 1865.

Sturt, Captain C., *Expeditions into Central Australia* (Adelaide Libraries Board of South Australia), 1965.

Taylor, P., *An End to Silence* (Methuen, Australia), 1980.

Telegraph Stations of Central Australia – Historical Photographs (Northern Territory Government Printing Office).

Treloar, A., *Further Extracts from the diary of Arthur Treloar* (unpublished).

Tolmer, A., *Reminiscences of an Adventurous and Chequered Career at Home and at The Antipodes* (Sampson Low, Marston, Searle and Rivington, London), 1882.

Tyler, M.J., Twidale C.R., Davies, M. & Wells C.B., *Natural History of the North East Deserts*; (Royal Society of S.A.), 1990.

Wilkes, G.A., *A Dictionary of Australian Colloquiallisms* (Sydney University Press), 1978.

Index

www.ingramcontent.com/pod-product-compliance
Ingram Content Group Australia Pty Ltd
76 Discovery Rd, Dandenong South VIC 3175, AU
AUHW020910100725
413679AU00003B/68

9 781743 056851